PRAISE FOR LE

With insight, humor, and tenderness Allan Ament's *Learning to Float*,

...offers a guide to how we might make such a journey with grace, love, and compassion.

....offers a wealth of inspiration and guidance for all who care for those they love in times of change, challenge, or illness.

... offers an intimate, humorous, and heart opening guide for embracing, honoring, and transforming how we respond to the inevitable sufferings, challenges, and precious gifts that life offers us as caregivers for those we love.

....offers an intimate, humorous, a compassionate, and inspiring guide for gracefully embracing the vulnerability of deeply sharing our lives and our love, while knowing that our cherished life together will inevitably end with some blend of illness, debilitation, and death.

> Joel and Michelle Levey, pioneers in hospice and palliative care training, founders, *Wisdom at Work*, authors, *Living in Balance, Luminous Mind*, and *The Fine Arts of Relaxation, Concentration, and Meditation*.

Ever wonder what the man is thinking? So much care-giving memoir is written from the woman's point of view... finally *Learning to Float* offers a male perspective-and what an authentic, vulnerable, heartfelt, spiritual warrior this man is. I loved how Allan Ament allows us into the marriage that was and the marriage that is, writing honestly about the love that bridges through his wife's profound stroke. A read for which I am most grateful and a story that will stay with me a long time.

> Christina Baldwin, author of *Storycatcher, Making Sense of our Lives through the Power and Practice of Story*.

A moving, sometimes heartbreaking, sometimes funny, always unabashedly honest account of Allan Ament's experiences over almost a decade after his wife has a massive stroke. It is a tribute to the resilience of two people suddenly faced with what Ament calls a "new normal." It is also a guidebook to getting past fear, grief, anger, hopelessness, and radically limited physical and cognitive abilities, sustained by love, determination, inquisitiveness -- and finally, again in Ament's words, learning to appreciate the amazing opportunities for life lessons we are given.

> Riane Eisler, author of *The Chalice and the Blade, The Power of Partnership,* and *The Real Wealth of Nations*

As a nursing professor of 30 years, I want this book to be required reading for every nursing student who hopes to care for patients and their families. I wept and laughed with Allan throughout yet as a nurse I saw moment after moment when a nurse could have made a difference had she just intervened as she had learned to do. Care is indeed like water, calm at times, rough at others and *learning to float* is a requirement for survival. And like water, care is essential for life. I love this book; it is well written, concise and wonderful to read.

> Eileen M. Jackson, Phd. CNS, RN, author of *Care is Like Water*

Allan's insights into the struggles of caregiving for a spouse are a useful read for anyone in his position. The book exemplifies the notion that stroke and recovery is not always just about the survivor, it is about how caregivers, family and the community react and learn how to deal with the effects of the event.

> David Wasielewski, The Stroke Network Book Review

A deeply felt and insightful memoir about how illness changes and challenges a marriage as well as the two remarkable, resilient people in in.

> Jane Adams, Ph.D., author of *Boundary Issues*

While the memoir is as much an account of caring for a loved one and is focused on Ament's experience in tending to his wife's needs, there is a universality in the narrative that should touch readers. . . .

With a natural flow in narrative and an ear for the senses, Ament paints three-dimensional scenes and recreates realistic dialogue to fully draw in readers. Beautifully paced and detailed throughout.

Lori A. May, Examiner.com

This author can really tell it like it is. He gives voice to all the people who are family caregivers. . . who may think they aren't handling things like they should. He helps you to know that the frustrations or feeling that come when faced with this life change are very real and okay . . . I was touched by the love he has for his wife, and the willingness he had to change and understand her better. Great to hear the man's point of view.

Jeweleo, BarnesandNoble.com

I was going to write that anyone who is currently the caregiver for a loved one should read this book. However, I am amending that statement. This book should be read by every adult. . . . [M]y advice is to buy and read this book as soon as possible, and hope that you never find out first-hand what Allan experienced.

Amiesbookreviews.com

LEARNING TO FLOAT

LEARNING TO FLOAT
MEMOIR OF A CAREGIVER-HUSBAND

ALLAN AMENT

ABIDING NOWHERE PRESS
GREENBANK WASHINGTON

Cover Design by Melody Barber
Edited by Patricia D. Eddy and Margaret Bendet
Photographs by Fredericka Foster Shapiro

Quotation by Eckhart Tolle From A New Earth: Awakening To Your
LIfe's Purpose by Eckhart Tolle, copyright (c) 2005 by Eckhart Tolle.
Used by permission of Dutton, a division of Penguin Books (USA).

Quotation from Ken Wilber from Grace and Grit, by Ken Wilber, ©1991,
2000 by Ken Wilber. Reprinted by arrangement with The Permissions
Company, Inc., on behalf of Shambhala Publications Inc., Boston, MA.
www.shambhala.com

PRINT ISBN 978-0-9854967-4-6

Library of Congress Control Number 2014919868

For Deloris, the love of my life and my teacher in all things. Your patience, love, and understanding is more than I deserve

TABLE OF CONTENTS

The human brain is a highly differentiated form through which consciousness enters this dimension. It contains approximately one hundred billion nerve cells (called neurons), about the same number as there are stars in our galaxy, which could be seen as a macrocosmic brain. The brain does not create consciousness, but consciousness creates the brain, the most complex physical form on earth, for its expression. When the brain gets damaged, it does not mean that you lose consciousness. It means consciousness can no longer use that form to enter this dimension. You cannot lose consciousness because it is, in essence, who you are. You can only lose something you have, but you cannot lose something that you are.

-ECKHART TOLLE, *A NEW EARTH:*
AWAKENING TO YOUR LIFE'S PURPOSE

To float: To move easily and lightly

American Heritage Dictionary

PREFACE
ON FLOATING

MY FIRST childhood swimming lesson was learning to float: how to relax and rest on top of the water. I learned if I didn't give in to my urge to struggle, the water would support me. I would be able to breathe. The human body is composed primarily of liquid. If, as Darwin posited, we humans evolved from waterborne creatures, we have the capacity to be at home in the water. Humans, however, have neither the gills that would allow us to breathe underwater nor the lung capacity of certain marine mammals to remain submerged for long periods of time. To breathe in the water, we must learn to float with our heads above water. Once we have mastered this skill, we can learn to move freely and easily in this alien medium.

A leaf rides on the top of the water, regardless of whether the surface is smooth or rough. Ducks and other seabirds surf the waves, gently adjusting their position to compensate for wave action and currents. Eagles, hawks, seagulls, and other birds ride air currents; their wings spread to take advantage of the air's movement, keep them aloft, and propel them to their destination.

These beings make no attempt to adjust winds or tides to more desirable levels. By riding the supporting currents of whatever is given, they achieve their goals. Learning to float, we survive. Taking the lead of the ancient Chinese spiritual masters Lao-tzu and Chuang-tzu, who use the flow of water as the Tao's principal metaphor, the philosopher Alan Watts called this universal path the Watercourse Way. By following the Tao, which Watts described with terms like the flow and the drift, we can live in harmony and alignment with our surroundings.

Water is also the image adopted by educator Peter Vaill, who coined the term permanent whitewater to describe business conditions that are "full of surprises," situations which were "never even imagined," with "novel problems" and events that are "messy and ill-structured" and "extremely costly." To deal with such conditions, Vaill advocated continual self-improvement: the need to see learning not as an occasional goal, but as a way of being.

This is also how whitewater rafters and kayakers approach their chosen sport. When facing a set of rapids, they study the flow of the river to maximize the potential of their encounter with the next rapids—as yet unseen but waiting beyond the bend. Rafters do not fight the current. Rather, they work with it. They ride this potentially dangerous force. They have learned to float.

In late August 2005, it was my turn. Deloris, my wife of eighteen years, suffered a stroke. She spent the next two months in in-patient care, progressing from the medical wing of the hospital to a skilled nursing facility to an intensive in-patient rehabilitation unit. Throughout this time, I commuted daily from our home on Whidbey Island in Washington State to various mainland medical facilities in Everett, a trip that required a ferry ride and took at least ninety minutes each way—more when traffic was bad or the ferry overloaded.

Deloris needed full-time, around-the-clock care when she returned home. Without hesitation or even conscious thought, I became her primary caregiver. I moved from being husband and friend to the woman I loved to being her guide, definitely a whitewater condition. To succeed, in fact, to survive, I would have to learn to float.

Several days after Dee's initial hospitalization, I began sending daily emails to family and close friends. It seemed the easiest way to get news to people scattered across the country. As the days morphed into weeks and other people heard about Deloris's condition, my distribution list grew longer and the geographic reach wider, spanning North America into Africa and elsewhere. The nature of the emails also changed from news about her condition to something deeper and more reflective. I began to write about how I felt, what I was experiencing, how my outlook and attitudes were changing, and what I was learning. More than a news brief, my emails became a personal journal—and a way for me to stay afloat. Sometimes people responded, offering support and appreciation, asking questions, or merely thanking me for their inclusion in my distribution list. I appreciated their messages and, at the same time, I did not expect any response from those who received my emails. In fact, I didn't even care if they read them; I realized I was writing the posts primarily for myself, to clarify in my own mind what was happening and what I thought and felt about it. If others found value or interest in what I wrote, that was an added plus. It was not, however, what motivated me to write, or to send out what I wrote.

My cyber-journaling continued for at least five years after the stroke. In semi-regular emails, I chronicled the external and internal journeys I traveled from being Deloris's husband, life partner and soul mate to also being her cook, laundryman, chauffeur, dresser, crutch— in short, her full-time caregiver. Nothing in my previous life prepared me for this—not practicing law, not teaching university classes, not owning a small business, not even parenting. Certainly not being a male! Not surprisingly, as I later learned, the majority of unpaid family caregivers are female. The reasons for this gender differential are varied and not really important to my story. I am male, and I became a caregiver for my wife, a position I embraced. It was full of heartache and pain, anger (mine) and love (ours), interspersed with moments of laughter. Our love and our commitment to each other grew and flourished in the fertile soil of Deloris's need and dependence. I found inner strengths I did not realize I possessed, and experienced fierce angers as well.

Finally, I realized the lessons I was learning needed to be shared. Mine is not a unique story, except in so far as I am an unpaid male caregiver. This presented some challenges and emotional obstacles others, especially females, may not face. (They will of course have to deal with their own unique challenges and obstacles). My hope is that my account of the journey I've undertaken may help others facing similar challenges. Perhaps from my story, and from the guidelines for floating I have learned, they may find clues that will help them learn to float. At the end of each chapter is one of the original emails. As much as I was able to do so, I chose emails that related to the relevant time frame, as indicated by the date of the email, or material discussed in the preceding chapter. I had hoped to have Deloris's voice more personally represented in the book. I asked her if she wanted to write a foreword, to which she agreed. Unfortunately, the residual cognitive damage she is dealing with made her following through on this commitment in a meaningful way impossible. She was, and remains, an excellent writer, a creative form which gave her incredible personal pleasure, as well as her readers. The absence of her words in this book is one of the many losses we share.

CHAPTER ONE
STRUCK DOWN BY THE GODS

The Chinese Dogs

SOMETIMES A SEEMINGLY nonsensical sentence can, in hindsight, become an omen of major life changes. Such was the case late one August morning, when my wife called from the bathroom, "I can't get up until I find the Chinese dogs. I know they're here somewhere."

We didn't have any dogs, much less Chinese ones. Hearing my wife talking nonsense, I knew I would not spend this Sunday morning watching pre-season football on television. Rather, we would be taking the ferry from the island on which we lived to the mainland, returning to the Providence Medical Center ER where we had been the day before. Deloris's condition had not improved overnight.

I needed to get her out of the bathroom, dressed, and into the car for this journey. Having lived through the '60s, I had some personal experience with altered states of consciousness. Placing myself as best I could into her reality, I said, "I think I saw them by the bed. Let's go look." Then I added, "You know, it's a funny thing about Chinese dogs. If you're dressed, you have a better chance of finding them."

"Oh, okay," she said placidly.

My ploy worked. We moved from the small bathroom back into the bedroom. "If we have some difficulty finding the dogs, perhaps we can go back to the ER. The doctor may be able to help."

"Good idea," Deloris agreed, much to my surprise.

Once she was dressed, I guided her, one labored step at a time, from our second floor bedroom to the main floor of the house, out the front door, and into the car. Every step she took was hesitant, made with difficulty. I was not overly concerned. I knew she wasn't well, but

I figured we could deal with it. How serious could it be? The day before the doctors had diagnosed Deloris with a urinary tract infection and dehydration.

Hours later, I sat in the ER cubicle, waiting for Deloris's test results. A young doctor dressed in green emergency room scrubs entered and in a flat, professional monotone, said, "Your wife's had a stroke."

I heard the words but could not absorb them. Nothing in the past twenty-four hours, or at any time earlier in my life, had prepared me for that pronouncement.

"We won't know the extent of the damage until we run some additional tests," he went on. "We can do that tomorrow. Tonight, we'll get her temperature reduced and monitor her condition."

A thin curtain separated the doctor and me from the other examination cubicles, now empty of patients. Institutional gray paint covered the walls. There was little light but considerable ambient hospital emergency room noise. None of it seemed real. Surely I wasn't receiving life-altering news. This young looking stranger in hospital garb talking to me, a stethoscope slung around his neck, file folder in hand, couldn't actually be a doctor. Yet as much as I wanted this to be a scene from a TV show, I knew it wasn't. It was real.

Your wife's had a stroke. I had never experienced so strongly the effect mere words could have. They knocked the breath out of me. I was totally unprepared for the doctor's pronouncement. His detached professionalism did not help. It was not his wife who had suffered the stroke, not his life that had been turned upside down.

* * *

Deloris had been feeling ill for a week. She'd had a slight fever, been unable to hold down food, and spent a great deal of time sleeping. By the end of the week, however, she said she was feeling better. She asked if I wanted to accompany her to Oak Harbor, a forty-five-minute drive from our home to the north end of Whidbey Island. She was going to conduct an interview for a newspaper article she was writing. A retired art and restaurant critic for The Seattle Times, the city's major daily newspaper, Deloris liked to keep her hand in and regularly wrote freelance articles. The drive to Oak Harbor didn't much appeal to me. I declined the invitation and suggested to Dee she probably wasn't well enough in that moment to drive herself.

She wanted to go and started for the front door, but before she got there, she stopped. "This is foolish," she said. "It's a long way to drive, and I don't need to do this interview right now. I think I'll go back to bed."

The next morning she was incoherent and unable to get out of bed. I phoned her HMO's on-call nurse who performed telephone triage. While Deloris's condition seemed serious, neither of us considered it an emergency. The symptoms were consistent with a urinary tract infection, something she'd experienced a number of times before. The nurse recommended I take Deloris to a walk-in clinic on the mainland, her HMO's closest non-emergency facility.

After a brief initial examination and an EEG at the clinic, Deloris was transferred to a nearby hospital whose medical staff had access to more sophisticated equipment and resources. Another exam and a subsequent CAT scan confirmed she was running a high fever, had a UTI, and was dehydrated as a result of her inability to retain much food or liquid. No cardiovascular or heart involvement was noted. Other aspects of the diagnosis could account for all her symptoms. IVs were put in place to rehydrate her with saline and administer antibiotics to lower her fever.

I was concerned by her condition but not overly anxious by the diagnoses. Thankful I'd brought a book, I attempted to get comfortable in the hard plastic chair the hospital provided for guests of patients and settled in for a long afternoon wait for Deloris's temperature to return to normal. When I couldn't concentrate on what I was reading, I watched the ever-changing numbers and lines on the readouts monitoring her oxygen intake, respiration, and other vital signs. I didn't understand what I saw but was entertained by the ever-changing visuals. Deloris lay on a padded examination table, covered by a number of thin hospital blankets, her skin cold to the touch even on this warm August day. Her apricot-colored hair was splayed around her paler-than-usual face, her eyes closed, her appearance serene as she slept. The beeping of the monitors and the ambient noise from an active emergency room helped to distract me from my concerns.

As the IV's liquid dripped into her body, Deloris became less feverish, more coherent. Life returned to her previously deadened eyes. When her fever finally broke, she was released to return home. With some difficulty, I helped her back into her clothes and onto her feet. As she stood, she collapsed into my arms, semi-conscious.

"Nurse!" I yelled. "I need help here. My wife."

Rushing into the room, a nurse helped me get Deloris back up on the table. The IVs were reattached, and the hydration process started anew. I settled back onto the chair and into my book, a bit more concerned than before.

After the IVs had completed their second drip, the doctor said he wanted to admit her overnight for observation. Deloris indicated she wanted to return home. After confirming I could get an antibiotics prescription filled, the doctor reluctantly acquiesced. He told Deloris if she could walk to the door, she could leave. Slowly, deliberately, leaning on me for support, she rose from the bed and shuffled to the door—weak, unsteady, but highly motivated. Back home, we slowly climbed the fourteen stairs to our bedroom. I helped Deloris into bed, propped her against a pillow, gave her a fruit smoothie, and went downstairs for a glass of wine, confident our hospital adventure was over.

Less than twenty-four hours later, we were back in the ER. This time the news was dire.

While I waited for Deloris to be settled in her hospital room, I began calling family. Each time I relayed my message, I cried, unable to speak without reliving the pain I felt when I first heard the diagnosis. "Deloris had a stroke," I sobbed to her siblings and to my brother. I left similar tear-soaked voicemail messages for the close friends who didn't answer their phones. Even when speaking into a recording device, my voice cracked under the emotional strain.

After the last call, I turned off my cell phone, unable to have any more telephone conversations. Now to the next order of business: I realized I had to be strong. I had to do whatever it took to get Deloris, to get both of us, through this experience. I had no idea how hard it would be; how much I would learn about myself, about my wife, about my friends. Locating the energies that would buoy both of us, using these currents to stay positive and move ahead, were my primary responsibilities for the foreseeable future.

For years I've taught organizational leadership to doctoral students. In my classes I constantly remind students that everything is a learning opportunity. Here I was, about to start the most challenging of postgraduate work I'd ever even contemplated. I knew I'd need to hone my skills for this, but I wasn't even sure which skills would be called on. I'd have to stay conscious, be super-aware, until I caught on.

Tears on My Pillow

Deloris and I had met twenty years earlier, in the mid-1980s, at a party given by mutual friends, Ben and Fredericka. It was the first Saturday in May, the opening day of sailing season in Seattle and, in my childhood home of Louisville, the annual running of the Kentucky Derby. Opening Day is celebrated by a parade of yachts, which pass by our friends' waterfront home. It's an opportunity for friends to gather, enjoy food, drink, each other's company, and the spectacle of watching highly decorated boats pass by. It was also a day when displaced Sons and Daughters of the Bluegrass, Louisvillians like myself, even those with no particular interest in horses, can celebrate their heritage by drinking mint juleps, the traditional drink of the Derby, and watching the horse race on TV.

I arrived at Ben and Fredericka's, having already consumed several juleps and carrying with me the fixings for more. After greeting my hosts and several friends, I went upstairs to the TV room where I knew people had gathered to watch the Derby. "Anybody want a mint julep?" I asked. Heads swiveled in my direction and hands were raised. I took a count and headed downstairs to prepare the drinks. When I had finished, I returned upstairs and distributed them to everyone in the room except one woman who seemed surprised by my return and my actions.

"You were serious?" she asked, surprise mixed with disappointment in her words. "What do I have to do now to get a julep?"

Through alcohol-hazed eyes, I looked at this woman whose reddish-blonde hair, falling in a pageboy and bangs, framed an attractive face with clear, intelligent eyes. I didn't know her but felt an immediate desire to do so. "You have to be very, very nice to me," I replied.

"Okay," she said, and followed me downstairs.

Using the beverage exchange as an excuse to introduce myself, I mixed another julep, handed it to her, and said, "Enjoy. By the way, my name is Allan."

"Thanks. I'm Deloris. I'm an old friend of Fredericka's."

"Me, too," I replied. "Nice to meet you."

* * *

Two years later we married, neither for the first time. Both of us considered our previous relationships, whatever their legal status, as practice for this main event.

Deloris made me laugh and, like me, took joy in intelligent conversation and wordplay. We shared a desire to understand how things worked and what ideas meant. In slightly varying degrees, we were both attracted to the offbeat, the arcane, the eccentric. We both loved to read, although usually in somewhat different genres. We appreciated similar movies and television shows and were both engaged in spiritual explorations. Our collective taste ran more to cats than dogs, Asian art more than European, progressive Democrats over conservative Republicans. We liked foreign travel, Thai food, good wine, and Mexico.

There were also lots of differences and, on the surface, we may have seemed a surprising couple. Raised in a close and happy family, I was instilled with self-confidence from an early age. Deloris's family background, though loving, was a bit dysfunctional. Following her mother's abrupt disappearance from the family when Deloris was ten, she and her siblings were raised by a number of aunts and a less than loving stepmother.

Also the difference in our ages meant we had different cultural memories. Eight years older than I (she was fifty-three when we married, I was almost forty-five,) Deloris grew up before the age of rock and roll and was a productive adult by the time the '60s rolled around. As a pre-teenager in the early '50s, I listened to Black rhythm and blues on a powerful out-of-town radio station and never lost my taste for the bluesy roots of rock and roll. I had a Black blues band playing at my bar mitzvah party, was one of the few Caucasians at both a Little Richard and an early James Brown concert, and heard Jimi Hendrix play the National Anthem on the Fourth of July at the Atlanta Rock Festival. Deloris, on the other hand, loved classical music, especially opera. This difference in musical appreciation resulted in an early agreement we made whereby she would not have to go to sporting events with me, and I would not have to accompany her to the opera. In spite of the times we violated this agreement voluntarily; it has held us in good stead throughout our relationship.

Spiritually, we were on similar paths. While I was born and raised Jewish and had developed Buddhist overtones in later life, Deloris was born Methodist, raised in part by Mennonite relatives, followed her own path to Buddhism, and was considering conversion to

Judaism when we met. She ultimately achieved this goal shortly before we married. Belief was more important to both of us than rote practice or blind faith.

Our differences were more than superficial. Inherently shy and introverted, Deloris always preferred solitary endeavors—reading, writing, watching TV. Socially, she is most comfortable interacting with close friends or small groups of people. Parties with large numbers of people, or mostly strangers, have always made her uncomfortable. On the other hand, I enjoy being in sizable groups of people. While I also like small, intimate dinners, I am completely comfortable with larger numbers of people sitting around my table or in my house. I am happy when my friends get to know each other and conversations become stimulating and highly interactive because diverse opinions are being expressed.

To accommodate our different social tolerance levels, Deloris and I often took separate cars to parties. Early on we agreed that neither of us had to go somewhere just to accompany the other. This is another agreement that helped our relationship thrive.

In many ways, I found the differences between us to be instructive. One difference that caused some issues over the years stemmed from the manner in which conversations had been conducted in our respective childhood homes. My mother had a temper that flared often and dissipated quickly. I inherited this tendency and developed an admittedly aggressive manner of presenting my thoughts and opinions. This style had been honed through collegiate debates, political activity, law school Socratic educational techniques, and years of being a trial lawyer. I never thought of myself as being verbally aggressive or seeking confrontation and was, in fact, often consciously uncomfortable with it. When Deloris and I met, however, I was considerably more competitive than I was willing to acknowledge.

Deloris, as I've said, is basically quiet. She dislikes confrontation and raised voices.

Eight years after we married, one disagreement stands out in my mind. Deloris exercised a quality of hers I cherish: an uncanny ability to identify a personal dynamic. Deloris and I were sitting across from each other in our living room, each with a glass of wine, recounting our days. This was a common end-of-day activity for us, one we liked to indulge in when no meeting, social engagement, or other evening activity demanded our attention or time. I don't remember the specific topic of conversation or exactly what I asked that elicited Deloris's response. Her response, however, I will never forget.

"Why are you cross-examining me?"

"What do you mean? I am not cross-examining you. We're sitting here having a drink, talking about our days, and I asked you a question." In my mind, I was visualizing the courtroom in which I had spent the earlier part of the day. A witness, under oath, had attempted to avoid making damning admissions under my questioning. This was not how I interpreted the conversation with Deloris, but I apparently had said something she took amiss.

"I feel like you are cross-examining me, and I don't like it."

"I'm sorry. I don't want you to feel uncomfortable talking to me."

As I've said, I knew Deloris disliked confrontations and raised voices. In my childhood home, exchanges with my mother often were done at a volume somewhat louder than a person's normal "inside voice." The tone was not meant to connote animosity or anger; it was for emphasis. Or, I don't know, maybe such volume was cultural. What I came to realize was that similar exchanges in Deloris's childhood home, if they took place, probably had different connotations. Whatever the cause, Deloris's accusation shook me. I had no desire to bring my work persona home, especially when doing so could negatively impact the relationship with my wife. While I didn't have the luxury of immediately processing the conversation to its fullest, I knew her comments were a sign I should re-evaluate how I lived my life. I did that, and Deloris's perspicacity turned out to be the catalyst for a major transition. I mark this conversation as the beginning of the end of my career as a lawyer, which happened only a few years later. My transition from the law—and from the constantly competitive, combative stance it necessitated for me—was the most significant shift of my adult life and, in some unforeseen ways, made this latest change in circumstance a lot easier to handle. If truth be told, it is also a transition I still struggle with maintaining.

Leaving the law is not a decision I ever regretted; it was one I think I had been contemplating taking almost from my first day in law school. I started law school almost by default—I didn't want to be a teacher, especially in higher education, science was never a strong suit, and going into the workforce was not attractive. And there was this war in Vietnam I had no interest in joining. I began the practice of law, as many lawyers do, with a strong sense of idealism and a desire to see justice done. That didn't last long. While I enjoyed some of the theatrical aspects of criminal defense and trial practice, the nature of that practice was combat, and my professional relationships were frequently confrontational. That wasn't what I wanted in my marriage. As I thought about it, I understood that it wasn't at all what I wanted in my life. The clarity of Deloris's comment, which brought into focus for me this disparity between what I wanted and what I was living, is something for which I will be forever grateful.

This is the nature of our relationship, and now, after eighteen years of marriage, I was faced with the possibility of losing it—losing my partner, my friend, my love.

* * *

In the weeks following Deloris's stroke, I quizzed her care providers and spent hours on the Internet doing research in an attempt to learn all I could about my wife's condition. Initial diagnostic tests indicated that the cause of the stroke was a right middle cerebral arterial clot. The cause of the clot was unknown. After her fever receded and the infection was controlled, the medical staff was able to determine the extent of damage and develop a treatment and rehabilitation plan. The damage appeared less extensive than it could have been. There was no blockage of arteries or internal bleeding. Deloris could swallow and speak. She was aware of her surroundings, although she had difficulty recognizing anything on her left side and was easily distracted by anything that crossed her visual field. She always recognized me and knew who I was. She remembered George W. Bush was president and how she felt about that unfortunate reality. These were all good signs, I thought. I learned through my research that most of a stroke victim's recovery occurs in the first three to six months, although continued recovery can take place for years.

When asked about causes, Deloris's neurologist told me, "We're unable to determine the cause of a stroke in about thirty-five percent of the cases. In fact, I'm not even sure your wife had a stroke, although it is the best possible diagnosis."

"What else could it have been?"

"Possibly a tumor or maybe some sort of infection. The MRI pictures of her brain don't really look like a stroke. The image of most strokes looks like a slice of pie, affecting only one hemisphere of the brain. Your wife suffered something, probably a clot, in the right middle cerebral artery, and most of the involvement is near that spot. It also looks like something happened in the left hemisphere as well. The picture of the involved area, however, does not look at all like a pie slice. Whatever happened, however, the treatment protocol at this stage is the same. So, we'll just monitor her condition and see what, if anything, develops."

Some part of me was perversely pleased the neurologist could not provide a specific diagnosis. He had been presented with a puzzle he could not readily solve. This intellectual challenge would pique his professional curiosity, motivating him to maintain a personal interest in her case until he solved the puzzle.

Brain attacks; cerebrovascular accidents (CVAs); apoplexy; strokes. I was learning a new vocabulary and amassing new information as I researched Deloris's condition. I gained a profound respect for the depth of information available through the Internet and the ease with which it could be retrieved. After culling what I considered baseless and what I didn't understand, what remained was impressive both in quantity and quality.

The various names attached to the condition reflected differing perspectives on it. It is an unexpected event, an accident, in the cerebrovascular systems, hence a CVA, or a brain attack, the commonly used medical terms. The term stroke was derived from a translation of the ancient Greco-Roman descriptor apoplexy, which refers to the sufferer as one who has been violently struck down by the gods. The term stroke seems have been introduced at the beginning of the seventeenth century.

Lifestyle and genetic factors influence the probability of a person suffering a stroke. Hypertension (high blood pressure), age, unhealthy cholesterol levels, smoking cigarettes, and diabetes are all risk factors. Yet, as the neurologist noted, about thirty-five percent of strokes occur with no identifiable cause. According to the American Heart Association, more than 700,000 Americans each year suffer a stroke. It is the third most common cause of death in the United States after heart attacks and cancer. Strokes are more common among older people, with ninety-five percent occurring in people over forty-five, and sixty-seven percent in people over sixty-five. They can occur in anyone regardless of age.

Deloris had several of the risk factors. She was seventy-one when the stroke occurred. Her cholesterol levels were high, and she was prone to migraines, some with auras, more risk factors. Some years after they reunited, Deloris's mother suffered a major stroke that left her unable to move or speak. On the other hand, Deloris didn't smoke cigarettes, suffer from diabetes, or have hypertension.

Whatever the etiology, the clot in her right middle cerebral artery cut off the flow of blood to the brain, thereby killing brain cells. Among its other functions, the brain's right hemisphere controls the left side of the body. Deloris's cognitive abilities were impaired, especially short-term memory and what are termed executive functions: decision making, organization, and follow through. Her speech and swallowing abilities were unimpaired, as those functions are more prone to damage in strokes occurring in the brain's left hemisphere. While she incurred no paralysis, Deloris suffered muscle weakness, joint and muscle pain, and an inability to use the left side of her body fully. Immediately after the incident, she seemed not fully aware her body had a left side, nor was she conscious of anything that happened on that side. Known as left-side neglect, the condition is neurological, not physical, in nature. It gradually eased during Deloris's recovery, and she became able to make the necessary neurological connections.

A stroke resulting from clots is termed an ischemic stroke or embolic stroke. This is distinguishable in causation from a hemorrhagic stroke, which results from a burst blood vessel causing bleeding inside the brain. The American Stroke Association reports that ischemic strokes are the most common, accounting for up to eighty-three percent of all strokes. Given the complexity of the human brain, no two strokes are alike. While the general nature of strokes may be similar, the consequences can vary dramatically. Numerous factors, including the affected location in the brain, the time elapsed before treatment, and the nature of the treatment received all contribute to the consequences of a stroke. Deloris's CVA seemed to be of moderate severity, and she received appropriate treatment within hours after the stroke was noticed. This gave me cause for hope, a buoy onto which I could latch.

I spent that first week at the hospital, returning each evening to our Whidbey Island home to recharge. I needed to gaze at the water and mountains visible from the house and yard. I needed to re-energize myself in the quiet of our neighborhood and cuddle with our cat Lydia. My first night alone, however, was not a peaceful experience. The house felt abandoned, empty of a part of its life energy. I was qualitatively different from the person who left the house earlier that day. I don't remember how I got home that first night. I must have been on automatic pilot, pointing the car in what I thought was the right direction and hoping that it, like a well-trained horse, would find its way back to the ferry terminal and then to its garage. When I left her hospital room, Deloris was asleep, looking nothing like the vibrant and beautiful woman with whom I had shared two decades of life. Granted no one looks their best in a hospital gown with wires and IV tubes extending from their body. Yet as I watched her lie there, slack-jawed, pale, expressionless, in a drug- and stroke-induced unconsciousness, the enormity and uncertainty of the situation swamped my mind. Not knowing was awful. I could not help but grieve and imagine the worst possible futures.

Once home, after feeding the cat and eating some dinner, I sat on the deck with a glass of wine. I hoped the silent beauty of the star-filled late summer night might calm me. It didn't.

Later, alone and lonely in bed, I cried myself to sleep, the first of many such nights.

September 6, 2005

Dear Friends of Deloris,

This is the first of a, hopefully very short series of emails giving periodic updates of Deloris's condition. Please excuse the impersonal nature of this type of communication, but it is the easiest way for me to communicate with all of you. I will be more than happy to talk with any of you on the phone as well. First, some background – Deloris suffered a stroke last Sunday, August 29th.

For about five days before she was diagnosed, she was sick with some sort of virus. She spent Saturday in the ER, where they ran a bunch of tests (including a CAT scan,) all of which were unremarkable except for showing she had an infection. She was running a fever and was dehydrated. On Saturday night after being rehydrated, given IV antibiotics and having her temperature reduced, she was released to go home. Sunday morning, I awoke to find her sitting in the same position in which she had fallen asleep the night before. She was drifting in and out of our collective reality. So, it was back on the ferry and to the ER in Everett, where she'd been the day before. In preparing to admit her, in order to treat her infection, dehydration, and temperature, another CAT scan was done which showed a small blockage in the right medial cerebral artery. All subsequent tests (an echocardiogram, blood work, Doppler test of the carotid arteries) indicated no further damages or blockages. She was able to swallow, was aware of who she and I were, where she was, and who the president was (and that she was still upset about that.)

Deloris spent the rest of last week in the hospital being treated for her infection and fever, along with therapy for the conditions caused by her stroke. Her appetite returned, although she willingly ate food of a nature and quality that ordinarily would never have passed her lips. So I knew that she was still sick!

The medical team is guardedly optimistic about her chances for a full and complete recovery. They indicate that it is too early to know anything definitive yet. How well she responds to therapy in the next few weeks will give some clues. To the extent that I can do so, I hold only an image of full recovery. To facilitate you doing the same, I am attaching a photo of her, taken at her birthday party last year, a happy time for her. I hope it is not too large a file—some aspects of technology are beyond me. [The photo and others are included later in the book.]

Deloris says she is bored, a good sign, and expresses an interest in having visitors. While she wanted some magazines, I don't think she is capable of sustaining the attention span that reading will require. I am also not sure she is able to connect the letters on the page with the meaning of the words. She was able, however, to fill out a form indicating beverage preferences and legibly sign her name. She indicated she wanted it all, operating on the theory that if the choices are either A or B, choose both. So, while she in not presently the greatest conversationalist, she has retained her sense of humor.

She is in Room 317, in the Bethany at Pacific facility, located in the Everett Providence Hospital Medical Center. If you call her, do not read anything into the fact that she does not answer; she may be asleep or, more likely unable to figure out how to answer the phone. You will also have to tell her to hang up the phone when you finish talking, as she has trouble figuring out how to do things. She is responsive to instructions, however.

Please keep her in your prayers. Send positive energies. Feel free to pass this information on to anyone you think might be interested. I will send periodic updates. If you do not want to receive them, please let me know. I certainly understand. If you know of others who might wish to receive them, let me know that as well, and I will add them to the list.

Your support, prayers and love have been a blessing this past week. Thank you.

Allan

CHAPTER TWO
LOOKING FOR BALLAST

To Ask for Help Is to Give a Gift

"WHAT CAN I DO to help?

"What do you need?"

As the news about Deloris spread through our Island and Seattle communities, friends immediately began asking what they could do to offer support. "Send positive thoughts and prayers for her recovery" was my initial response.

I couldn't think of anything else I needed, other than having my wife returned to her normal self. Near the end of the first week, a different answer became clear. I needed food. I had neither the time nor the energy to shop and cook. It was late each night when I returned home from the hospital. While I was hungry, all I wanted to do was unwind. I didn't want to worry about cooking something. Being able to give a specific response to my friends' questions led to the first of many lessons I was to learn. I could not do this all by myself. I had to ask for help.

Initially, I found the asking hard. I grew up in a caring community and lived in one now. My mother was a social worker, so I knew about giving assistance; requesting and accepting it, however, was a different story. I grew up in the 1950s, instilled with the American spirit of self-reliance. Asking for help implied inadequacy. It was an admission that I was not self-sufficient. I struggled with the dilemma raised by the ideals of independence and self-reliance juxtaposed against my belief in community and collaborative efforts.

My friend Barbara told me, "Look. Asking for help is giving your friends a gift. You are allowing us to do something for you. If you don't ask for help, you deny us this opportunity. You like to give gifts. Do it."

This reframing resolved my internal conflict. It gave me permission to figure out what I really needed and ask for it. Despite this, the first time I asked was very difficult. The response my request elicited, however, made successive times easier.

"I need food," I emailed. Within hours, someone had posted a schedule asking people to sign up to deliver meals at specific times. In the ensuing weeks, I arrived home from the hospital to find meals waiting on my doorstep. In the previous years, I had been a vegetarian and then an Atkins diet devotee. Now, I enthusiastically welcomed whatever food showed up. My culinary preferences and previous dietary restrictions were no longer important. Anything ready to eat was wonderful. The potential for leftovers was even better. If it appeared at my door, I ate it. Worry about my diet was relegated to a time when an issue that insignificant could once again demand my energy and attention. Meals prepared with care and compassion, I felt, would overcome any empty calories and increased carbohydrates.

Sometimes I found homemade soup and salad; other times, meat loaf, mashed potatoes, and pie. Notes of support and expressions of concern for Deloris, a joke, or maybe only a name, were tucked in among the plastic containers. Some of the cooks were old friends; I knew others only by name. A few were people whose faces I might have recognized but whose names were unknown to me; perhaps they were friends of Deloris's or friends of friends. I felt blessed by the physical nourishment the food provided, but even more so by the emotional support from these friends and friends of friends who cared enough to take the time and effort to prepare food and deliver it to me.

Perhaps people who live on an island develop a sense of interconnection not necessarily present in an urban environment. Years before, when I lived on Bainbridge, another island in Puget Sound, my house burned down. Luckily no one was injured, although I lost almost everything I owned. Within hours, without ever asking for help, I was surrounded by donations from friends, community members I'd never met, and church groups. As word spread throughout our island community, people responded, knowing that while I was the one in need that day, it might be any of them tomorrow. The circumstances around Deloris's stroke were different in that the loss was far more personal and could not be replaced by well-meant donations. Yet the desire to help, to support Deloris and me in our time of need, was the same. I felt blessed to live on an island and to be held by my community.

Whidbey Island, home to about 45,000 people. Twelve to fifteen thousand (the number varies dependent on the source) of them live on the south end, where Deloris and I live. The island is beautiful. Surrounded by water, with snow-capped mountain ranges visible to the east and the west, scenic views are everywhere. Eagles, hawks, osprey, herons, and other smaller songbirds nest in the evergreens; deer and rabbits roam freely terrorizing people's gardens. Small farms dot the landscape, the resident cattle, horses, and sheep lending a bucolic overtone to the scene.

Many of us who live on South Whidbey Island feel we are part of a special community. It is not a sense of superiority, but rather one of being lucky, of being blessed, if you will. I came to Whidbey, as I have described it to friends, "kicking and screaming." Years before, Deloris and I had bought a house on the island both as an investment and a weekend retreat. I loved its location across the street from the beach. My experience with that house was less than enjoyable. I now recognize the reasons had nothing to do with the house or Whidbey Island. When we finally sold the house, I told Deloris I was done with Whidbey; I never wanted to step foot on the island again. Eight years later, however, I was living full-time on the Island and grateful to my wife for making it happen.

South Whidbey, while predominantly inhabited by Caucasians, is diverse in many ways. In addition to Christian churches of every major denomination as well as some more minor ones, South Whidbey is home to both a Zen Buddhist monastery and a Tibetan Buddhist one, as well as a Quaker community, Sufi practitioners, a nascent Jewish community, and Wiccan practitioners. A small two bed hospice, associated with the Zen monastery, provides end-of-life service to people of any or all religious beliefs. Residents tend to be older, often retired, commuting to the mainland, or working from home, there being few employment opportunities available on the South End. There are, however, at least three theater companies, including an active Whidbey Children's Theater, not to mention the performances put on by the schools. A number of choirs and other musical groups, a small orchestra and other organized ensembles provide musical performances of every genre. Glass artists, painters, sculptors, and other visual artists practice their endeavors alongside writers, musicians, film-makers, dancers, actors, story-tellers, and creative sorts. People are friendly and helpful, once one makes an effort to meet them and ask for help. The sense is one has moved to Whidbey to be left alone; when that assumption is shown to be erroneous, the community opens and the newcomers are absorbed. It is not quite like the Borg on Star Wars ("Resistance is futile; you will be assimilated.") as the assimilation is voluntary and only to the extent desired.

In addition to the artistic endeavors common on South Whidbey, there is also a strong community focus on environmental sustainability, community interdependence, and creating a safety net for those in need. The local food bank supplies needed food; groups of people prepare sack lunches for school kids who can't afford to buy their mid-day meal, and others make soup for adults who want a hot meal. Local nonprofits assist in helping with medical bills, transportation, housing, and other necessities. For the most part, the over 400 nonprofit organizations serving our small community grew organically and operate as neighbors helping neighbors, with the understanding that tomorrow the roles might well be reversed.

This time it was my and Deloris's turn to be helped. And helped we were. I wanted to thank everyone, and since my first request had gone so well, I-half in jest-wanted to see what would happen if I mentioned the rest of my wish list. "The food is wonderful," I said in my email. "Thank you. Thank you. Y'all have done such an incredible job leaving me delicious meals, and I am incredibly grateful. This has taught me that when I ask for something there is a possibility I will receive it. So, here goes. I need chocolate, really good red wine, gasoline and ferry tickets!"

What the hell, I thought. It's certainly worth a try. If nothing else, maybe it will give some people a laugh. Within days, chocolate bars and chocolate tortes appeared at my front door alongside bottles of red wine. No gasoline, but someone left me a book of ferry tickets.

When I commented to Barbara how overwhelmed I was by people's response, she replied, "I told you your asking us for what you need is a gift to your friends. Remember that."

Accepting this perspective became an important lesson.

In the weeks following Deloris's hospitalization, my life settled into a routine. I spent days at the hospital, sitting with Deloris, and advocating for her care with the medical staff. Hours passed on my cell phone conveying information to friends and family. My talks with Deloris were frustrating. She had always been a wonderful conversation partner, highly intelligent, with the quick, inquisitive mind of a journalist. Now, she struggled to find and form words.

Scraps of overheard conversations, irrelevant and often nonsensical phrases, as well as bits from television shows she heard became incorporated as part of her personal history, relayed to others in her recitation of her daily events. Deloris's grasp on the reality most of us share was tentative at best. She tended to combine her perception of what was actually happening around her with snatches of past memories, television sound tracks, overheard conversations, and dream realities. This mixture was often more interesting than what was "normal," making it easier for me to join in her reality than to attempt to bring her into the one the rest of us shared. I was thankful my earlier experiences as a hippie made it easier for me to relate to and accept alternative realities, both mine and others.

Often when I arrived at the hospital, I found Deloris sitting in a chair, reading a book. Before her stroke, when she wasn't writing, she was usually reading. The woman loved to read; she loved words, her own and those from others. Since she made her living as a writer, this was not surprising. Now, however, her reading was more of a pantomime of her former activity. She sat in a chair, or in her bed, a book in her hands, looking at the same page for minutes, if not hours. While she could read the words, I don't think she was able to comprehend their meaning. The mere act of having a book in her hands, and her eyes gazing at print on a page must have been comforting to her, as it was certainly familiar.

Watching Deloris eat hospital food with relish was clear evidence to me that she was not her former self. Food items that this former newspaper restaurant critic would not previously have touched were now thoroughly enjoyed. When the nutrition staff asked for her menu preferences, Deloris operated on the theory that if the choices are A or B, one should choose both, especially when the subject was dessert. That she was able to keep her sense of humor and her priorities (sweets, especially chocolate) in this time of trauma was an encouraging sign. In the days and weeks to come, I needed all the encouraging signs I could find.

As I sat with her at dinner, watching her consume unidentifiable dishes she often referred to as "pre-chewed food," I remembered a conversation we had years before. I was reading a review she had written about a new Seattle restaurant we had eaten at several weeks earlier. In addition to being art critic for The Seattle Times, Deloris often wrote book reviews and periodic restaurant reviews. I was able to join her for many of these meals, much to my delight, as I do like to eat. I don't remember the name of the restaurant whose review I was reading, or exactly what Deloris had written about our meal. I do remember neither of us thought as highly of the food or the service as she had indicated in her article.

"Did we eat at the same restaurant? Was I with you?" I asked. "I don't remember liking this place that much. Your comments during dinner were a lot more critical than this."

"Yes, you're right," she said. "But I think it's important to say positive things whenever I can. People's careers and professional lives can be ruined by some casual comment by reviewers more concerned about their own reputation than the hard work and dedication the restaurant staff have put in. I don't want to be that critic; I am not that kind of person."

I wondered if Deloris's change in culinary preferences was commonplace among stroke victims. A review of information on the Internet disclosed primarily anecdotal evidence of appetite and taste bud changes at all ends of the culinary spectrum. Like other post-stroke issues, the medical evidence I could find indicated that these changes would most likely resolve themselves during the initial recovery stage. The degree of resolution, of course, would depend on the severity of the stroke, its location, and other variables. As I would later observe, in Deloris's case, her changes resulted in an initial increased desire for sugar, especially in the form of chocolate, and then, years later, in a marked increase in the amount of time it took her to finish eating a meal. None of these issues were especially troublesome to me.

Deloris was inherently kind, both professionally and personally. It was one of the things I loved about her. She was a considerate critic, careful of the feelings of the artists, writers, restaurant owners, and chefs whose work it was her job to review. It was not her style to impose her own sensibilities and preferences onto others' creative works.

"My role as a critic is to help my readers understand what the artist was doing in his or her work. I may like or dislike a given piece, depending on my own artistic sensibilities. But, as a writer, I know how much effort goes into the creative process. Just because I don't happen to like a given piece of art, a book, or a dish of food doesn't make it bad. It just makes it not to my liking. Other people may like the piece of art; the chef may have had an off day or the dish contained ingredients I personally don't like. Someone else may really like that dish. When I encounter something creative I don't like, I don't feel that makes the work bad. My personal tastes are not the criteria by which I judge the creative work of others."

This approach to her work as a critic gave her both credibility with her readers and the respect of those whose work she wrote about. At the same time, when she believed the work she was reviewing was substandard, she had the vocabulary and the creative ability to convey this opinion, supported with facts in such a way that her comments reflected only on the work and not on the creator. Everything she did was done with personal integrity. Not only did I love her, I was incredibly proud of her.

Connections: Family and Friends

Celeste, Deloris's only child, flew in from Rhode Island as soon as she heard the news. This was an especially happy event because the two had been estranged off and on for many years-the reasons buried in a family history of real and perceived hurts.

Deloris had married Celeste's father while still in college. Shortly after Celeste was born, Deloris realized the marriage had been a serious mistake, one she had to correct if she was to thrive as a person. As a condition of the divorce, Celeste's father demanded Deloris give up custody of her daughter. Deloris reluctantly agreed. So, when Celeste was two, Deloris left the family, recreating her own family-of-origin story. When Deloris was ten, her own mother had left her family, her desire to escape an abusive relationship trumping the love of her offspring. For Deloris and Celeste, attempts at reconciliation over the course of the ensuing decades achieved only short-term détentes.

I first met Celeste about fifteen years after Deloris and I married. We had traveled to Ohio, where Celeste lived, to visit Deloris's daughter, grandkids, and great-grandkids. During that visit, I enjoyed witnessing a renewed connection begin between mother and daughter. The two carved out time for private one-to-one sharing.

There were hugs and handholding as well as looks filled with love and affection. Plans for additional visits were made. Yet after a short post-visit period of contact, old habits resurfaced and communication between the two ceased. Deloris was initially hurt, not understanding why Celeste failed to respond to calls, notes, and emails. Ultimately, she became resigned to the situation, accepting the loss as a replay of her relationship with her own mother. I am sure Celeste similarly grieved the loss in her own way.

Knowing this family background, I debated whether, and how, to tell Celeste the news about her mother's stroke. I concluded Celeste had a right to know. A few days after the event, I called her and left a message on her voicemail. "Celeste, this is Allan. I don't know if you care, but your mom had a stroke. She's in the hospital. We don't know yet how serious her condition is."

I didn't know how, or even if, Celeste would respond. I was surprised, and pleased, when she called back a few hours later, saying she would be on the first possible plane.

An attractive fifty-year-old with blonde hair, a Rubenesque figure, and a hearty laugh, Celeste was a trained, experienced, and enthusiastic caregiver. Throughout her visit, she was at her mother's side early every morning, giving me a much-needed break and the two women an opportunity to reconcile. Celeste's attentive response to Deloris's needs and requests clearly demonstrated how appreciative she was for this chance to care for her mother. Perhaps she was moved by Deloris's incapacity. Perhaps she was motivated by the fear that her mother might die before past injuries were healed. Or perhaps the fact that Celeste was experiencing estrangements from her own children, similar to what she and her mother had gone through, may have made the need to re-establish a connection with her mother all the more important. Whatever the impetus, we all were gratified by its results.

Whenever I entered Deloris's hospital room, the love and caring between mother and daughter were evident. Celeste sat by the side of the bed, lovingly brushing her mother's long reddish-blonde hair, its usual luster dulled by days spent in a hospital bed. As her daughter patiently worked the tangles from Deloris's hair, the flat unemotional affect that had been her normal post-stroke look eased. Her eyes showed life and awareness.

Rational conversations with Deloris were still difficult, as she spent only short periods of time in our collective reality before retreating to the scenarios playing out in her injured mind. Celeste handled this challenge with grace and aplomb.

"Do you remember when that person came into my room yesterday and asked where they were filming the movie?" Deloris asked.

"Yes," Celeste said, though the conversation had taken place on a television show the two had watched the previous morning. "We gave him directions to the fourth floor, and he thanked us."

Deloris nodded, satisfied, as if the scene was replaying in her mind.

Even without the benefit of rational and extended conversations, Deloris knew who Celeste was and was moved by both her presence and her caring ministrations. This initial re-knitting of mother-daughter ties helped both their healing processes. I was deeply touched by what I saw and heard.

Deloris's sister and brother-in-law also flew in from Denver to be with her, as did our friends Ben and Fredericka, who were then living on the East Coast. Deloris deeply appreciated their presence; their love and energy seemed to energize her. While social interactions tired her, especially those in late afternoon, the positive energy these visits generated undoubtedly supported her. I was grateful for their presence, both for Deloris's sake and for the respite it provided me.

In the middle of these visits, I met Dr. Eric Gehrke, the neurologist assigned to Deloris's case by her HMO. A pleasant man in his early forties, he seemed professionally competent and personable, with a cheerful and friendly bedside manner. I liked and trusted him almost from the instant I met him. Fortuitously, he had met Ben earlier that day. A physician and biochemist, Ben was a former department head at the University of Washington. Dr. Gehrke had studied under one of Ben's good friends, a fact uncovered in a quick "Do you know . . . ?" exchange between the two. That personal connection moved Deloris from being just another patient on his caseload to a specific human being, a transition I believe had positive ramifications over the coming months.

After a brief neurological examination and a review of her file, Dr. Gehrke was encouraged about Deloris's long-term recovery prospects. Deloris had suffered a decline during the previous days, becoming increasingly lethargic and unaware of her surroundings, which I found troublesome. The doctor assured me that this was a normal pattern for people who suffered strokes similar to hers. The regression was usually transitory, as it was with Deloris, and of no real significance. I wished I'd had that information earlier, as it would have eased my anxiety.

Deloris's condition required extensive rehabilitation and medical care and would for some time. Our previous lifestyles, both individual and collective, were dramatically changed, perhaps permanently. About ten years before, Deloris had retired from two decades as a newspaper art critic. She continued writing on a freelance basis. In addition to incisive book reviews and art criticism, she had authored four books, including Iridescent Light, an award-winning overview of the Northwest School of Art and its proponents. At the time of her stroke, she was revising a novel that had garnered interest from several agents. Her disability put this integral aspect of her prior life and self-identification on hold.

Recreational travel, something we previously enjoyed, would also be curtailed. Our prior journeys together had taken us to China, Sri Lanka, Nepal, Bali, Thailand, Costa Rica, and Mexico, as well as San Francisco, New York, Louisville and Ohio, the latter two locations for family visits. Deloris had made reservations for an Antarctic cruise later in the year. I was sure we would not be going on that cruise. I didn't know when, if ever, we could again enjoy going to the movies, spending time with friends, mushroom hunting in the woods, restaurant dinners, occasional evenings at the theater, and the spontaneous day trips which had been a normal part of our previous life. For the foreseeable future, a trip off to the mainland for medical appointments with side excursions to Costco and Trader Joe's would be a major expedition.

About a week after her initial hospitalization, the neurologist thought Deloris had progressed sufficiently to be transferred to a skilled nursing facility within a day or two. When I told Deloris about this option, she wondered if we could do it in Hawaii. I laughed at her response but began to fantasize the possibility. We loved Hawaii, having visited a number of times and considered relocating there. Going there now for rehab, however, was not a feasible option.

Barring any relapse, the initial medical aspects of Deloris's treatment were over. The focus now was on rehab-helping Deloris relearn walking and thinking, rebuilding the neural pathways necessary for leading a quasi-normal life. The goal was to assist her to develop the highest degree of functional independence her damaged body and brain were capable of attaining. For Deloris, the hard work of becoming her former self was about to begin in earnest.

Even given the darkness of the circumstances, I was buoyed by the love and support emanating from family and friends. Their presence provided some ballast at the beginning of this journey that allowed me to breathe easier, gather some energy, and prepare for what lay ahead. It is not always obvious that positive things can flow from the tragedy of a loved one suffering a stroke. Yet they can. This realization was, and continues to be, a large part of my experience. The genesis of the mother-daughter healing I witnessed was directly attributable to my wife's condition. While only a tangential beneficiary of that interaction, I was a more direct recipient of lessons resulting from friends' responses, and their offers of help when they learned of Deloris's stroke. My attempts at learning to float were buoyed by the knowledge I did not have to go through this alone.

"Lawyers Don't FEEL!"

In the gray warmth of an October evening four weeks after Deloris's stroke, I sat on our deck, a cup of coffee in hand, and reviewed my life. It had been three years since we moved to Whidbey Island from Seattle. It was a transition I had resisted, but was happy I had let Deloris talk me into making. It was also one month short of three years since Deloris's Aunt Kay moved in with us, at age eighty-nine, to spend the remainder of her life. After several heart attacks, the aftermath of a massive right brain stroke had ended her life five months before. Without conscious intention on my part, caregiving had become constant in my life. I'd had no real preparation for this role; both my parents had died suddenly, obviating the need for my brother and me to care for them. I was trained as a lawyer: a left-brain, rational being.

I hadn't dreamed of becoming a lawyer when I was young. Who does? Like many boys of my generation, my career fantasies ran more to being a cowboy. Academically, I had an aversion to science and medicine. My family expected me to get an education and a profession. There was no family business to inherit. I didn't want to be a teacher or college professor, and I had a strong desire to avoid military service in Vietnam. I liked to talk and argue, so law school seemed a logical alternative.

My first day of law school remains indelibly etched in my mind. With about two hundred classmates, I sat on an unpadded wooden chair at the back of a long rectangular classroom, writing tables rising on three sides, forming a deep well in the middle of the room. The instructor stood behind a podium in the well, disdain evident on his face. I think most of us were excited to be embarking on this journey toward what we hoped would be a fulfilling and lucrative career, and a bit anxious about what lay in store for us. I certainly was. The teacher stared at us for a few uncomfortable and quiet moments before he spoke: "Clear your desks. Take out a piece of paper and a pen. This is a test."

I was incredulous. What could he be testing us on? Is this what the next three years held in store? Oh . . . I remembered. He had given us a pre-class reading assignment. I had skimmed it, not understanding much of what I read. Now I discovered I didn't know the answers to most of the questions we were asked. This provided me with my first lesson in law school: read the assignments. The second was this: make yourself as invisible as possible when the instructor is looking for someone to call on in class. Lesson number two was especially important on those occasions when I had not followed lesson number one.

During the course of the next three years, I was academically and intellectually challenged in ways I never experienced before in my life. I learned to "think like a lawyer, talk like a lawyer, and write like a lawyer," as one of my professors described the transformation the law school faculty was attempting to bring about in their students. The problem was that once they had done their job, we-the students-were capable of conversing only with other lawyers.

Another apparent law school initiation rite I'll never forget involved my contracts professor, one of the eldest faculty members, who looked considerably frailer than he apparently was. Using a textbook he had written, the professor attempted to teach us the intricacies of contract law, one of the foundations of the profession. He assigned court opinions from his book for us to read (all of which, we subsequently learned, had been selected because of the erroneous decision reached by the judges.) In class, he called on students to discuss the assigned cases by summarizing the facts, the issues before the court, and the judges' reasoning. When the student's presentation was finished, the instructor would ask a series of questions and pose "what if" scenarios, probing the student's understanding of the court's decision. Once the student had been drained of all knowledge and reasoning, the professor would move to another sacrificial lamb. This Socratic questioning was the standard pedagogy in all of our law school classes.One day, early in our first semester, a student began his recitation by saying, "I feel the judge . . ." The professor slammed his hands on the podium, his face turning an unnatural shade of red, and roared, "Lawyers don't feel! Lawyers think!"

Like my classmates, I feared the professor's apoplectic reaction was going to put him into cardiac arrest. We later realized this was a routine he went through with each first year class. Early in the semester, some student would always say, "I feel . . ."giving the professor the needed opening to make the only point I remember from his class: lawyers don't feel; lawyers think! It was the last time any of us used the verb to feel during the three years of our legal education. It may well have been one of the last times we experienced any emotion, at least in our professional capacity. It would take me years of therapy and time away from the practice of law to regain contact with this part of my emotional being.

Now, years after law school and my departure from the practice, I sat on my deck, overcome with feelings of fear and emptiness, part of me wishing I had been a better law student and learned not to feel pain. While I was a good student, I was also an emotional creature and was grieving the loss of my mother, as it was the eleventh anniversary of her death. Like Deloris's stroke, that earlier tragedy came without warning; like Deloris's stroke, it made me realize the importance of friends and family. The death of my mother, coming ten years after that of my father, was also the first time in my life I truly felt like an adult. I had no parent to turn to, no relative who could "make things right." I had to be responsible and self-reliant. If Deloris was to get better, if we were to have anything approaching a normal life, even a new normal, it was up to me. I had to marshal my inner strength, to gather the resources and assistance I needed from others, and to focus on helping Deloris.

Doing anything else never crossed my mind; she was my wife, my soul mate, and she needed my help. Of course, I would be there for her. I would use my intellect, my rationality to learn and master the skills and knowledge I would need to care for her. I would use the love and gratitude as sources of energy to keep me afloat through this journey. And I would accept the help of others. I was extremely grateful for the loving support from our friends. I cannot fathom how anyone can go through something like this alone. Once I experienced the results of asking for assistance and felt how powerful the sense of needing others, and accepting their help, could be for both parties, it became easier. What a gift!

September 16, 2005

Thanks to everyone for bearing with me as I go through my emotional roller coaster ride in quasi-public. I certainly don't mean to inflict my pain and frustration on others, but I have always been a member of the "if I am hurting, everyone around me will know it" school of suffering. It's no fun doing it alone.

Dee was somewhat better today- she was alert and verbal, able to stand up and move a short way on her own with the help of a walker. At least when the therapists were working with her. She ate well, and showed some culinary discrimination by passing on what was described to me by the nutritional aide as not very tasty dry French toast. Salmon and spinach linguini, however, was a hit for dinner. Too bad the staff thought she was kidding with her requests for a pitcher of martinis. (While she probably was, the nurse and I thought it sounded like a good idea.)

Dee's daughter returned to the East Coast, carrying with her a new appreciation of her mother, some self-realizations, and a couple of bottles of Whidbey Island Winery's finest as a present for her husband. It was wonderful having her here. Dee's sister and brother-in-law returned to Colorado today as well. It was a good visit.

Frustratingly, Deloris will not be returning to Whidbey Island anytime soon. It appears that the South Whidbey doctors who contract with Group Health do not share in the same sense of community obligation that bonds the rest of us. Of course, theirs is a professional decision, driven by ethical (and perhaps economic and other) considerations. The result, however, was that no physician was willing to take medical responsibility for her. All this would have required of a doctor is to see Deloris a couple of times a week, if that often, at Whidbey General Hospital and to be on call if some emergency arose. Consequently, Dee will not be on Whidbey for rehab; rather, she will stay in Everett.

Needless to say, I am less than happy about all this. The Providence discharge counselor and the Group Health liaison are equally frustrated. I am sure the doctors involved all thought they had legitimate reasons for refusing, including, of course, that none had a doctor-patient relationship with Deloris (neither did any of the other five doctors she has seen since being in the hospital.) Whatever the rationalization, the result is that Deloris cannot receive care, medical and otherwise, in her home community, and I continue to spend at least three hours a day in my daily commute to Everett. I have no concerns about the quality of care she will receive at Bethany; when we were there about a week and a half ago, the staff was compassionate, attentive, and competent; the room was nice (and private-unlike Coupeville) and the facilities comfortable, if a little institutional. So, I have to accept what is happening as the only thing that can happen, and seek solace in the words of that great twentieth-century European philosopher Mick Jagger, "You can't always get want you want. . . but if you try sometimes, well, you might find you get what you need."

Today, I am working hard at not being angry with those Island doctors whose decisions impacted my life. I know frustration will not change their decision or give me the strength and energy to continue caring for Deloris. I know the love and support we are receiving from everyone else so far outweighs this inconvenience-for that is all it is-and to waste time on negative energies is counter-productive. Nonetheless, at some primal, animalistic level . . . .I gaze upon the yellow roses that were dropped off as food for my soul (along with food for my body), and I realize that what I need to focus on is the love and support Deloris and I are receiving. Negativity spawns only more negativity, and I cannot afford to live in that energy.

Besides, gas is twenty-five cents a gallon cheaper in Everett than on the Island, so there are some positive aspects to continuing the commute. Now, if I can just find a good, convenient Ethiopian restaurant. . .Life is precious. Tell those you care about that you care about them. Don't wait. And, since it is September, Go Huskies!

Y'all are wonderful, and I will be forever grateful!

Allan

CHAPTER THREE
SWEETS FOR THE SWEET

The Anniversary Waltz

SEPTEMBER 7TH is our wedding anniversary, a time to celebrate that lovely, hot, sun-drenched Labor Day in 1987, when, basking in the warmth of family and friends, Deloris and I were married. She looked elegant and lovely, dressed in a white Japanese wedding kimono, embroidered with red peonies and golden cranes as she stood on the deck of the decommissioned ferryboat on which we held our celebration. A garland of fragrant maile leaves, a gift from friends in Hawaii, was draped around her neck. A haku lei of white tea roses and green leaves encircled her head. Her smile, radiant below reddish-blonde bangs, did not falter when I dropped the wedding ring. Luckily, I was able to grab it before it sank through the boards of the aft deck into Lake Union. I grin each time I look at the image of Deloris smiling from the photo our friend Johsel Namkung took that day. The picture has a prominent place in my office and travels with me when I am away on business.

Eighteen years later, September 7, 2005 began with a call from one of Deloris's nurses "Your wife's hair has a major snarl in it. We couldn't get it out when we washed her hair. Is it okay with you if we take her to the beauty parlor we have here on-site so it can be cut out?"

"Sure," I said, wondering why they didn't ask Deloris. The answer to that question, as well as the existence of the snarl in her hair, became moot a short while later when the nurse practitioner called back.

"You know Deloris hasn't been doing well since she arrived here," the nurse said. "We don't know what's wrong. We're transferring her back to the medical wing of the hospital for some tests. Hopefully, the results will give us some answers." My permission was not requested, leading me to think Deloris's condition might be more serious than the nurse's comments were meant to convey.

For the four days since her transfer to the skilled nursing facility, Deloris had lain in bed, semi-conscious, unable to move on her own. She couldn't generate energy even to watch TV or the birds and blue skies out her window. The transfer had occurred at the beginning of a long Labor Day weekend, when staff was greatly reduced. As a result, Deloris had received no physical therapy, minimal nursing care, and even less medical attention. I became increasingly nervous as I watched her regress. She talked little, ate almost nothing, and had less and less energy. Once the holiday weekend was over and staffing returned to normal, I voiced my concerns to the medical staff. Tests were ordered to determine why Deloris was on this downward spiral.

When I arrived at the hospital Wednesday, September 7th, our wedding anniversary, I was told the most recent CAT scan showed the stroke had impacted a larger portion of her brain than originally thought. No one was sure whether she had recently suffered another stroke or if the original clot had spread.

Concerned, and more than a little afraid, I attempted to hide behind a cheerful face when I entered Deloris's room. "Never let 'em see you sweat," as my trial practice instructor had taught me. "Are you in pain?" I asked her.

"Only when they stick me with needles or I attempt to move my head," she said. Her head remained cocked to her left most of the day. She had lost some additional strength in her left hand and leg. Sitting at her side, watching her sleep, not knowing the meaning or long-term seriousness of this visible downturn in her condition was nerve-wracking. It is one thing to understand intellectually the ebbs and flows of the healing process. I did well in that regard. It was a totally different thing to attempt to integrate this knowledge when it was my life partner lying in the hospital bed, wan and drained of energy.

After dinner, when I could no longer tolerate the anguish of being unable to do anything productive or helpful, I decided to go home. As I was leaving, the doctor on duty, whom I had never met, stopped me in the hall. "What do you want us to do if she codes tonight?" he asked, calmly holding her chart in his hand.

"What?" I was stunned by the question and initially unable to process the question. Then it came clear. "There should be directives in the file."

"There are. But what do you want us to do tonight if something happens? Should we attempt to revive her?"

"Of course." I realized this answer was contrary to the directive's instructions. I couldn't comprehend why the doctor was forcing me to deal with this issue, angry at being required to address this possibility, and appalled at what I perceived to be his insensitivity to what I was feeling. Fantasizing the possibilities that might trigger his inquiry nearly paralyzed me. I couldn't process the conversation nor come close to realizing that the doctor considered the question to be a routine part of his checklist. Later I considered that not having to deal with such decisions in a state of intense emotional stress was the primary reason we had filed advance medical directives. In the moment this doctor confronted me with his questions, I was too distraught by what these questions said about Deloris's condition to wonder why he just didn't rely on what he knew was in the file. I still don't know the answer to that question.

I walked semi-consciously to my car; with tears streaming down my face and I made my way home. Alone in bed, huddled under blankets, I celebrated our seventeenth wedding anniversary, worried—terrified—that Deloris might not be around for the eighteenth. Exhausted, I fell into troubled sleep.

The next morning, I was reluctant to leave the safety of the house with its calming view of Puget Sound and the Olympic Mountains. I dreaded having to face the unknown that awaited me at the hospital. The ferry trip was a blur, even though I usually enjoy this short time on the water in late summer, nourished by the warmth of the sun and the physical beauty of the area in which I am blessed to live. That day, however, my thoughts and emotions were focused elsewhere.

With trepidation, I entered Deloris's room. She was sitting in a chair, bright-eyed and alert, smiling and talkative, as if she had not a care in her world. "Hi, Love," she said. "Happy anniversary."

I was speechless, being both overjoyed and dumbfounded by this 180-degree turnaround in her condition. A nurse related that she and Deloris had been having a wonderful conversation about my wife's experiences as an art critic and her favorite artists and authors. Apparently large parts of Deloris's long-term memory were intact, and she was able to track conversations and participate appropriately. This seemed to bode well for the future.

It was the best anniversary present I could imagine.

Pie for Lunch, Wedding Cake for Dinner

"What would you like for lunch?"

Deloris didn't hesitate. "Pie."

"Just pie? Nothing else? A sandwich or salad?"

"Nope. Just pie. A piece of peanut butter cream and a piece of raspberry cream."

Deloris and I were at a sandwich shop on the Everett waterfront, accompanied by her recreational therapist. The excursion was part of a program to help my wife become socialized and reintegrated into the community in preparation for discharge from the hospital. It was the recreational therapist's job to facilitate the process, and this luncheon excursion was a first step. Deloris was able to walk from the car to the restaurant, read the menu, determine what she wanted, and give the waitress her order. Her ability to handle these seemingly mundane, but important daily activities with confidence and ability was encouraging. It demonstrated how much she had recovered in the six weeks since her initial hospitalization.

Deloris devoured both pieces of pie. They did look good. I rationalized that Deloris's lunch was nutritious since it contained protein (peanut butter), fiber (also from the peanut butter), vitamins (raspberries), and calcium (cream filling). Equally important was the pleasure of being away from the hospital and free to order and eat whatever she wanted, a freedom she found especially delicious.

When we returned to the rehab center, Deloris's first request was for me to escort her to the gift shop. She had chocolate in mind.

The day before this excursion, some friends had gotten married. When I received my invitation I had called them to ask if it included my wife. With obvious discomfort and more than a little embarrassment, they voiced a preference that Deloris not attend. They noted concern that their living room, the celebration's location, was neither wheelchair accessible nor handicap friendly. The crowd of people might make it difficult for Deloris to concentrate, which, in turn, might make her uncomfortable. While they didn't say this, I thought they also might not want the focus of guests, many of whom were good friends of ours, shifted from them as the wedding couple to Deloris. I assured them their decision was not a problem.

"Andi and Norman are getting married," I told Deloris. "The wedding is at their house."

"That's great!" she said. "I want to go."

"Of course," I said. "You need to know, however, there are steps leading into the house. The bathroom has no grab bars. And lots of people will be crowded into what you know is a small room. Are you sure you are going to be comfortable?"

"Oh." She thought about it. "Maybe not."

"After they return from their honeymoon and you're back home, let's invite them for dinner and some island time. That way we can spend some quality time with them. I'll explain you didn't feel comfortable attending, give them a hug from you. And do the same to everyone else who asks about you."

"Good idea."

So, a possibly awkward situation was avoided.

On my way to the wedding, I stopped at the hospital, carrying the couple's present. It was wrapped but needed a ribbon. My plan was for Deloris, our household's designated gift wrapper, to finish the job, making her feel more connected to the wedding.

"Find me some long leaves," she said.

"Why? What are you going to do with them?"

"I'm going to braid them into a ribbon and paint them." Apparently, once Martha Stewart has taken up residence in a mind, she doesn't leave—no matter what the circumstance. I struggled with how to get Deloris to simplify her approach and focus on the materials I'd brought and the short time frame we had. A few minutes later, she picked up a crossword puzzle and announced, "I'll wrap the present later." My observation that I was under some time pressure and didn't have time for her to do it later had made no impression; however, the crossword puzzles had caught her attention and the half-wrapped wedding present was no longer an issue for Deloris— another potentially awkward moment avoided.

I wondered how the shift of focus had come about. Was the puzzle merely a mental distraction? Had the crossword puzzle crossed her field of vision, causing her to focus on it rather than the task she had been working on? This was a common enough occurrence. Or was this change in activity a way of asserting a bit of independence, a bit of control over her now diminished life and how she spent her largely prescribed time?

Whatever the answer, I finished wrapping the present myself. The mental image of Deloris's concept of painted, braided leaves brought a smile to my face as I worked.

Driving back to the hospital after the wedding, I received a voicemail message from Deloris. This was the first time since her stroke she had called me. "Hello, this is Deloris. I want to talk with you. Please call me." Her voice was a bit hesitant as if she was uncomfortable speaking into the void that is voicemail. Almost as amazing to me as getting this message was the fact that she answered the phone when I called her back, also a first. "Please pick up some chocolate covered pecans and bring them to me at home," she said.

"I'm almost at the hospital and really don't have time to go looking for candy," I said. "I do have a surprise for you."

"Can I eat it? Is it chocolate?"

"You'll just have to wait and see," I said. "I'll be there in ten minutes."

When I arrived, she was in bed, reading her journal. "I'm tired," she told me. "I need to have 'lie downs' whenever I can. The therapists work me too hard!"

I laughed. After showing her pictures of the wedding I had taken on my digital camera and relaying messages of love and support from friends, I gave her the surprise—two pieces of chocolate wedding cake.

The cake quickly disappeared and Deloris went back to reading her journal. She ignored her dinner when it arrived.

"I've already eaten. I had wedding cake for dinner," she said when I asked if she was going to eat. Who could blame her for choosing chocolate wedding cake over hospital food? Eat dessert first; life is uncertain has always been her guiding culinary principle. And as her life was becoming increasingly uncertain, perhaps eating wedding cake for dinner meant her decision-making abilities were returning.

The week after the wedding brought another excursion and another culinary adventure. For weeks, whenever the nutritionist asked Deloris what she wanted to drink with dinner, her response was either a martini or a glass of red wine. Neither, of course, was available through the hospital's kitchen; nor did I think Deloris was totally serious. The exchange became a running joke. Now, Deloris was finally able to have a glass of wine with dinner.

We were at a waterfront restaurant having dinner with Ben and Fredericka, who were back in Seattle for a while. What made the evening memorable was not the conversation with old friends, or even serendipitously running into other friends at the restaurant. Rather, it was watching Deloris engage in previously normal activities, including ordering and drinking a glass of wine with dinner. Little variations can often result in more substantial changes. I was overjoyed by watching Deloris manage these rather routine activities with ease, something impossible for her to do even a week before.

At the same time, I was exhausted by the emotional ups and downs I was experiencing as I attempted to navigate the roiling currents of Deloris's recovery. It was similar to what I'd experienced the few times I rode a roller coaster. There is the initial excitement when settling into the car. As the coaster slowly climbs the first incline, there is the feeling, the hope really, that this isn't going to be bad. As I crest the initial rise and plummet down a steep incline, screaming in panic, I hope against hope the ride will be over quickly. Of course, it never is. There are more hills to climb, more descents and hairpin turns to careen through, more rapids around the next bend in the river to disrupt the calm enjoyment of life and scenery.

No matter how much I might wish the ride over, no matter how much I prayed Deloris would miraculously be returned to her pre-stroke self, I knew I would have to stay with this to the end, whatever and whenever that might be. I was here voluntarily, if not entirely of my own volition.

October 25, 2005

It took almost two months, but Deloris finally had a glass of wine with dinner! As with so many things, I am not sure that the actualization was as good as the expectation. However, Deloris seemed to enjoy the wine, as well as the outing. We were sitting at Anthony's in Everett, overlooking the Marina, having dinner, once again, with our good friends from NYC, Ben and Fredericka. The conversation ranged from Deloris's condition, especially compared to what it was the last time they were in town (when she was first in the hospital) to getting permits for house repairs in Seattle and to children and old friends. A not unusual menu of dinner conversation topics.

What I enjoyed most about the evening was not the conversation or even the time with friends, as delightful as both were. Rather, it was watching Deloris walk up stairs, open a door, enter a restaurant, sit down at a table, read a menu, and order dinner. It was seeing her able to do things that weeks, even days ago, would have been beyond her abilities. I was thrilled.

On the other hand, before we left, Deloris was not sure where she was. She couldn't understand why Lydia, our cat, would not come when she called. Deloris didn't realize she wasn't at home. This confusion about location has recurred in a number of different contexts during the past several days. In part, I think Dee is merely trying to make sense of her surroundings.

We are still on track for a Monday discharge. I have a meeting with her care providers on Thursday and training with the therapists on Friday. A meeting with the discharge counselor is also being scheduled. I'm as ready as I will ever be. I know Dee certainly is.

Some of you have asked for a picture of Deloris to use as a focal point for sending healing energies, so here's one taken at her seventieth birthday party several years ago. Thanks for asking, and for sending the energy.

Allan

CHAPTER FOUR
NEGOTIATING THE RAPIDS

Confabulations and Grammar Snobbery

DELORIS WAS EASILY DISTRACTED the entire time she was in rehab. She spent a great deal of time in worlds and time zones of her own creation. Time was not linear for her. She flitted backward and forward in time with equal agility. Some events she described having experienced actually existed only on TV or had been overheard in conversations between others. "Do you remember yesterday when that man came into the room asking if I had seen his sister? The one who had run away from the nursing home?" As she asked this, Deloris looked at me with concern, her desire to help the man evident in her expression.

"I remember you telling me about it," I said. "I don't remember seeing the man." On the contrary, I did remember both the conversation and the man's appearance, having seen and heard them on a television program only moments before.

Her therapists assured me this kind of nonlinear memory was normal behavior for people who've had strokes. The term for it is confabulation. Wikipedia describes this as "a memory disturbance, defined as the production of fabricated, distorted, or misinterpreted memories about oneself or the world without the conscious intention to deceive." Normal or not, this confabulation was initially difficult for me to handle. Even with my previous recreational drug- and meditation-induced experiences in alternate states of consciousness, I found myself unnerved when I heard what sounded like nonsense coming from my wife. I did, however, try not to display any evidence of my discomfort to Deloris.

Months later when Deloris was doing outpatient speech therapy and I was more comfortable with her confabulation, I asked her therapist to describe the most interesting incident of confabulation she'd experienced in her practice. She said that one day a patient of hers, a chef who had experienced a traumatic brain injury in a car wreck, asked her, "Do you remember when we were standing on the parapet of the castle throwing chickens down to the peasants below?"

Always looking for humor, I found myself wondering if the patient remembered what color dress she was wearing and whether the chickens were still alive.

Beginning a few weeks after her stroke, Deloris obsessively wrote down whatever caught her attention. Her notes evoked the same confusion of reality and fantasy, of television and actual events. Here is a sampling from one day, recorded here exactly as Deloris wrote them:

> Bedside Table w/ water cup, remote, lined notebook, blue pen
>
> Oct. 7 – What happened today? A few things fell apart–
>
> So: Prosthetic testicles for neutered dogs top today's list.
>
> Bless our Bush who "foiled" yet another plot. And I haven't the faintest idea what the man is on about.

The last note made me think she might be more lucid than any of us gave her credit for.

A friend lent us the latest Harry Potter book, which I began reading aloud to Deloris. We had enjoyed listening to the earlier books on tape, and I thought Deloris would enjoy this one as well. I'm not sure if the book led to increased confabulation or it was too hard for her to concentrate on my words. Whatever the reason, my reading to her was not successful. I gave up.

I spent my days at Deloris's bedside. I did schoolwork on my computer or watched daytime TV as she slept. Game shows, the Food Network, sitcom reruns, and baseball games filled time, demanding little or no engagement on my part. I wanted—needed—to be there, as much for my own emotional stability as for whatever my presence could do for her.

Her room was sunny, filled with light. Flowers from friends lined the windowsill: white orchids, yellow roses, purple dahlias. I regularly brought flowers from our garden for the nurses—grateful for the attention they gave to Deloris. What I brought Deloris was chocolate. Chocolate in a variety of forms filled available counter space and drawers in her room. To Deloris, chocolate was not a luxury but one of the major food groups and a medicinal product of great efficacy. I taped family photos, greeting cards, and other images to the wall opposite her bed in hopes they would bring some joy, as she realized how many people cared for her.

One day, I walked into her room and began to laugh. If spiritual energy helps the healing process, Deloris was covering all bets. She was in a Lutheran-run nursing facility, housed in a hospital administered by Catholic nuns. Depictions of Hindu deities and the Buddha were taped to the wall opposite her bed. Our rabbi and his wife were sitting in the room when I arrived. A Sufi friend had just left, and two of Deloris's Buddhist Dharma teachers were expected shortly. She had all her spiritual bases covered.

* * *

Days became weeks. Deloris's spirits were high; she seemed comfortable and content in the facility. At times, however, she disappeared from reality. Her eyes rolled back into her head, which was always cocked to one side. Her body trembled uncontrollably. When I touched her hands, they were cold; so were her feet. The outside weather was warm, the room temperature even warmer. Yet Deloris lay under several blankets, shivering.

I was concerned at this loss of body heat. Her neurologist thought she might be having mini-seizures and prescribed medication that, if effective, might also trigger increased memory retention. Unfortunately, none of the medications had the desired effect. The seizures continued, parts of her body twitching uncontrollably. I became increasingly concerned, and her doctors had no explanation for what was happening. Inexplicably, when the anti-seizure medications were stopped, so did the seizures.

My legal training, and natural tendency to research and analyze whatever confronted me was a great help in supporting Deloris. I searched the web, read numerous books and articles about what other caregivers experienced as well as what professionals recommended. I wanted to learn all I could about strokes, their symptoms, and consequences. Some of the resources I found most valuable are listed at the end of the book. I learned the difference between ischemic strokes (those caused by clots which obstruct the flow of oxygen to the brain) and hemorrhagic strokes (which result when a weakened vessel ruptures leaking blood into the brain), the latter seemingly having the more serious consequences.

I also struggled through dense, technical neurological studies, gaining a better understanding of brain physiology while reawakening prior knowledge about the functions of the brain's hemispheres and the role of cerebral arteries in supplying blood to various parts of the brain. In general, among other responsibilities, the right brain (the part of Deloris's brain damaged in her stroke) controls spatial orientation and integration, intuitive problem solving, as well as simultaneous processing. The left brain regulates mathematical functioning, analytical abilities, writing, and complex motor functions. The corpus callosum, a wide bundle of fibers between the right and left cerebral hemispheres of the brain, facilitates communication between the two.

All of this information was valuable, helping me to appreciate what I was going to experience when Deloris came home and providing suggestions on handling various issues that were apt to arise. Patience, hope, and humor were important traits for successful caregiving. Since I had no other training, this is how I prepared for what had become the next phase of my life's journey.

One morning, my quiet time at home was interrupted by a phone call from the duty nurse. "Deloris fell this morning and hit her head. We ran tests and no damage was indicated, other than a bruise on her forehead."

"How did it happen?" I asked.

"We think she had to go to the bathroom and wanted to do it without having to call for help. She tried to get out of bed by herself, and fell."

I certainly understood the motivation. What could feel more demeaning than having to ask for help to get to the bathroom as well as on and off the toilet each time you had the need? While the nurse and I agreed Deloris's striving for independence was a positive step, we both were concerned about the potential damage she could inflict on herself. I was relieved she was not hurt, and also exhausted by the emotional toll these ups and downs exacted. Floating was beginning to feel like drowning.

As I researched Deloris's condition, I also read about how caregivers need to take care of themselves first or they will not be able to care for others. This was a recurring theme I was to encounter many times over the next several years. I could feel the truth of it, although I was not ready to make any conscious efforts to implement changes in my routine.

My days were a blur of ferry rides and late nights. My emotions continued their ride down the rapids. I became hopeful whenever I saw signs of progress, however small. I plummeted into tear-soaked depths of grief and fear when the reality of present events and fantasies of a dark future overwhelmed me. I was exhausted in every way. It seemed to take all my energy to stay in the present, to avoid thinking about the future—which, as far as I could tell, would be filled with caregiving and a less than fully functional partner. If we were lucky.

* * *

Deloris spent much of her day "reading." Whether her mind absorbed what her eyes scanned remained a mystery to me. In fact, I never saw her turn the page in the book she held in her hands. She did seem to feel comforted by the familiar feel of a book. She also resumed writing in her journal, although she was unable to complete the memory exercises her therapist had given her. Like Deloris's conversations, the writings often incorporated what she had heard on television.

1-888-esurance.

Mouth-breathing Hick

Prom suit

"Happy Hand Club" $45 mill gross for Film

Eagle Mont in Burien – —luckiest place in state.

The Cat's Mask Inn—individual suites (gone fishing suite) $18/night.

Dogs have masters; cats have staff.

Jun Kim—Chinese winner of the "trip of a lifetime."

Even when it did not make much sense, Deloris's writing displayed some of the same command of language she'd had in the past.

Sherri's dad helped bail me out from assorted alarms for brussel [sic] sprouts,

Desserts, God knows what else and we hope tomorrow's Dreams will provide dream fodder.

Lord Knows, I'm ready for fresh dreams, even the Pepperidge Farm variety.

Or the Moon of Red Ponies.

And the "5 Worst Article Endings" (according to Writer's Digest and Stephen King. It all lies in ample use of sky blue (or as my dad would say, "sky blue pink".)

Reading her transcriptions reminded me of my experience in an undergraduate existentialism philosophy course long before word processors or electric typewriters. I had been up all night retyping the final version of a term paper, the radio blasting rock and roll to keep me awake. While I worked, the prescription meds I had taken to keep me alert began to wear off. As they did, I unknowingly transcribed minutes of a top-of-the-hour newscast into the body of my paper. I gave the unread final draft to my roommate to turn in while I went to bed. When the paper was returned, the instructor had circled the offending section in red, with the marginal note "brilliant." I received an A+ on the paper. It was, after all, an existentialism course, and the professor, a visiting instructor from Oxford University in England, had assumed the inclusion of the news was intentional. I said nothing to dissuade him, ecstatic with the grade and the future story potential of the incident.

* * *

"Can you believe this?" Deloris asked one day when I entered her room. She handed me a flyer passed out by hospital staff, publicizing an event for patients. I recognized Deloris's handwriting in the edits scrawled across the page. "All these grammatical and spelling errors. It's a disgrace."

Deloris's grammar snob persona had returned. She has always been one of the best copy editors I have ever experienced. Her comments about the handout indicated she was making progress in returning to her old self, even if this manifestation might be annoying to others.

Her speech therapist designed a new series of exercises into her therapy sessions to take advantage of Deloris's proclivity to edit whatever written material appeared before her. When she got all the answers right, Deloris beamed like a proud third grader receiving a gold star on a spelling quiz. I rejoiced in her sense of accomplishment, and at the same time, my heart broke. The achievements she was so proud of were the academic equivalent of that proud third grader. My extremely bright, highly erudite, gifted wordsmith of a wife—a woman whose past cognitive and intellectual skills always left me in awe—was celebrating being the intellectual equivalent of a nine-year-old.

We all learn, and relearn, new skills, one baby-step at a time.

I Can Take Rapids or Leave Them

The roar from unseen rapids filling the air above a slow moving river raft quickens my heart. This sound heralds unknown obstacles around the next bend that could propel my boat down the river or flip it upside down with potentially dangerous consequences. These existential fears, coupled with the probability for some adrenaline-releasing excitement, is why I raft rivers. I enjoy the thrill of shooting rapids in a raft, but I don't care much for the emotional ups and downs of a metaphoric ride. It would have been easier if I did, as the longer it took Deloris to recover, the more I realized this journey was going to be a long river rafting journey, often on Class Five white water—slow, calm drifts followed by unexpected, heart-stopping trips through the rapids, followed by stretches of calm water, followed by rapids and then calm stretches of quiet water, followed by . . . You get the idea.

About six weeks after her stroke, I was sitting with Deloris when a new speech therapist came into the room. The therapist introduced herself, obtained Deloris' agreement of cooperation, and asked a few preliminary questions. She then asked, "Can you write a sentence for me?"

Looking up from the book in her lap, Deloris said, "Sure. Do you want it in English?"

Both the therapist and I were surprised by the response. The therapist said, "Can you write in any other language?"

"I can write something in Spanish."

"Well, I'm going to South America for a vacation next month, so Spanish would be good."

I stood up and moved behind Deloris. Slowly and deliberately she wrote a long sentence in Spanish, which she translated: "If you see this woman on the street, treat her with respect. She is remarkable." Relying on college Spanish courses and some proficiency in restaurant Spanish gained on numerous trips to Mexico, I confirmed the accuracy of both the grammar and the translation.

When Deloris indicated the therapist was the subject of the sentence, she made a friend and ally. I don't think she did it with that intention. Throughout the recovery, she was without guile or hidden agendas, both being beyond her capabilities. She had written this sentence as if it were the most natural thing in the world to do. While she was somewhat fluent in Spanish, I had never known Deloris to write anything like this before her stroke.

I was thrilled at what I considered a clear demonstration that parts of Deloris's higher-level cognitive functions were operating, even if in unusual ways. I was so excited by her obvious progress; I forgot that life is not lived in a straight line—especially when you're recovering from a stroke. This reality became clear minutes later when Deloris's lucidity lapsed and she lost all interest in everything except the book open in her lap. All the while, her body continued its constant involuntary moving without intruding on her awareness or causing her any concern.

Days passed in this yin-yang atmosphere of hope and concern. The intensity of Deloris's condition was juxtaposed against the mundane nature of everything else. Meditation, walks on the beach, watching Marx Brothers movies, and writing the emails that began to serve as my journal entries as well as connecting me with friends and family and kept them abreast of developments—all of this buoyed me and, at the same time, helped me through the changes I was experiencing. While focused on the micro, I knew I needed a more macro-perspective if I were to help Deloris and maintain my own sanity. I had to learn to be emotionally present and involved while remaining detached and objective. I had to learn to remain above the emotional fray, for I sensed I would soon be in circumstances more challenging than anything I was presently experiencing or had experienced in the past.

Only a month and a half before, I had been concerned about Deloris' endurance to take a hike, her ability and desire to paddle a kayak, or complete a writing assignment on deadline. Now, I rejoiced when she was able to pull on a sweater over her head, to stand up with minimum assistance, or maneuver her wheelchair down the hall to the dining room without getting distracted by something on the wall. What a change!

One afternoon Deloris's neurologist called and reported, "Yesterday's EEG showed no surprises." The subtext to this statement was that he still had no idea what had happened to my wife. The specialists reviewing the images from Deloris's earlier CAT scans and MRIs, as well as the present data, were puzzled. Some questioned whether she actually had suffered a stroke, since neither the shape of the mass visible on the images nor her progress fit their ideas of what an ischemic stroke should look and act like. Of course, very little about Deloris had ever fit the standard mold, but that may well be another story and, at the same time, one of the reasons I love her.

The most recent EEG had unfortunately done nothing to resolve those uncertainties. Some other possible explanations for Deloris's condition—a virus, encephalitis, a tumor, or even cancer—made a stroke seem almost desirable. Deloris was, however, improving, unlike people suffering from these other conditions. So the alternative explanations remained only possibilities, rather than probabilities. It felt strange to find myself hoping Deloris had had a stroke.

The neurologist laid out four options for further diagnostic procedures. "We can assume she had a stroke and continue her present course of treatment. We can do a lumbar puncture (LP) to obtain spinal fluid to check for potential viruses and cancer cells. I can refer Deloris to a doctor at the University of Washington who is one of the country's top neuro-oncologists, or we can do a brain biopsy."

The biopsy was an extremely aggressive procedure, especially as it was for diagnostic purposes only. "No biopsy," I said. "If you think the LP might be useful, let's do it, and then set up a consult with your expert at UW."

When the lumbar puncture procedure turned up no cancer or viruses, the referral to UW was deemed unnecessary. The diagnosis of a stroke remained operative, and intellectual curiosity about the possible anomalies helped maintain professional curiosity and interest in Deloris's situation. I liked that.

When I looked at Deloris' condition as objectively and dispassionately as I could manage, I saw progress in some areas, less so in others. I didn't know if that was normal; hell, I didn't even know if there was a normal. She was becoming more mobile, yet she still could not walk without assistance. Her balance was shaky. She needed guidance and help to stand up. And the left-side neglect was still present. Her lack of executive functions made initiating actions difficult, if not impossible. While her speech and long-term memory appeared intact, there had been little progress with short-term memory or confabulation.

I didn't know what progress was normal for this stage of recovery. It was hard for me to judge my wife's level of improvement, as I saw her often and was emotionally involved in the process. I had to rely on my research, the perceptions of people who saw her only periodically, and on her rehab team for what I considered more accurate and educated assessments. I received mixed messages from them.

"There is no real norm." "Everyone progresses differently."

"Deloris is doing well."

"She had a bad day but is progressing nicely."

What was I to believe? The neurologist's continued uncertainty, coupled with his desire for additional testing, forced me to consider other, more drastic causes for Deloris's condition. As they were only theoretical, I tried neither to put any emotional energy into these nor to focus on worst-case scenarios. I really didn't care what Deloris's condition was labeled, so long as it was treated and she recovered. After all, what's in a medical label? A rose by any other name . . .

At the same time, the diagnostic uncertainty tipped my emotional raft down another trough, albeit less steep than earlier ones. I remained confident we would come through this whole and healthy. Yet, I really didn't know how it would turn out. I focused on Deloris's improvement in rehab. That was easy for me to do during the day when I was with her or working at home.

At night, alone with my thoughts, dealing with uncertainty and ambiguity, was a different story.

October 1, 2005

The last twenty-four hours have been a hell of an emotional roller coaster. Not much sleep last night as images of the enormity of the task that lay ahead of me interrupted slumber with tears and fears. Overwhelmed by the changes in my life that I perceived awaited me in the coming weeks, grieving the loss of what was, and could have been, and wondering where I will get the strength to deal with the new adventure. Finally, I got to sleep and awoke if not refreshed, at least prepared to face another day.

In the gray, damp light of the first day of October in the Pacific Northwest, I took refuge in the fact that many others I know, including close friends, have faced ordeals much more severe and longer lasting than mine. There is no doubt that Deloris will continue to improve; a full recovery is still within the realm of possibility/probability. She is not suffering from AIDS, ALS, a terminal disease or condition; she is not psychotic; she does not have degenerative MS and is not vegetating in a coma. She can do things; she is able to walk, although presently needing assistance; she can talk, laugh, tell jokes, read, write, and edit other people's writing. She knows who she is and who I am, which in many ways is more important to me. I realize that we have supportive friends and resources to cope with whatever occurs. The responses I have received after last night's posting have helped me put some perspective, intellectual if not emotional, into my/our situation. They have reminded me how blessed we are with friends.

None of us know what the future holds for us. The path on which I find myself is a journey into living in the present, into practicing mindfulness and compassion, into caregiving yoga. I have been raised to be of service to others; while I often thought of this as meaning others "out there," for the foreseeable future, the "other" to whom I must be of service is the one with whom I have chosen to share my life. So while amusement park roller coasters are not anything to which I am attracted, it appears that I will be riding an emotional roller coaster for the foreseeable future. I learn to allow the tears to flow when they well up, to find joy and laughter wherever I can, and learn to ask for, and accept, assistance from others. It is easier in the daylight than in the solitude of my bed.

This weekend marks the third anniversary of our move to Whidbey Island, a transition I will never regret. It is also the yahrzeit (anniversary) of my mother's death, an event that makes Rosh Hashanah (which begins Monday night) a bittersweet occasion in my life. Today, however, my thoughts are not about these events, but on Deloris. She was in good spirits today. We spent some time reading the Everett Herald, including a review of a new book of Yom Kippur readings and meditations, which was pointed out to us by the social worker at Bethany, the rehab facility in which Deloris is presently residing. Deloris told some jokes, laughed a lot, and was present and interacted appropriately with visitors. She seemed to be gaining insight into the seriousness of her condition, and recognition of the limitations she is presently suffering. This did not appear to make her anxious, angry, or depressed; rather, it was merely information, which she acknowledged with the same degree of acceptance that she greeted the news that she was getting better and should continue to improve.

Both her mind and her body (especially her hands) seem to be in constant motion. While it is fascinating to watch her mind work, it is somewhat disturbing to watch her hands move nonstop. Both, I think, are part of the healing process. While I know I should be taking steps to make the house safe for Deloris and beginning to think how I am to manage providing her with 24/7 care, I find myself able to focus only on the present situation. I accept this as a necessary momentary avoidance response, allowing me time to process what the future holds. Intellectually I know that Dee's return home will necessitate her being monitored, that she is still unable to operate independently. The reality of what this will entail, however, clearly did not sink in before her therapy team outlined it to me.

So, now I am processing both the cognitive data and its emotional ramifications. That will just take some time and then I will be able to go forward, at least until the next set of rapids.

Allan

CHAPTER FIVE
A DELICATE BALANCE - FOR DELORIS

What's All the Fuss?

WHEN THINGS WERE going well, Deloris approached her therapy with an attitude of "I don't know what all the fuss is about. Everyone can walk down the hallway or feed themselves."

Most of the time, however, whatever crossed her field of vision became the sole focus of her attention. This made walking down the hall, eating, or any other daily activity time-consuming, if not impossible. It could be the television, a picture on the wall, or even the lettering on the soles of her shoes. Once she was distracted, concentration on the task at hand was impossible. If someone attempted to refocus her attention on what she had been doing, Deloris often responded with the I-don't-want-to-and-you-can't-make-me attitude common in two-year-olds. According to her doctor, both this stubborn streak and her left side neglect were normal. They were, nevertheless, frustrating.

As she continued to improve, Deloris's medical team became more receptive to the suggestion of excursions. When the stroke first happened, I fantasized Deloris would be well enough to attend *Kol Nidre* services, which were to be held about six weeks later. *Kol Nidre* begins *Yom Kippur*, the Day of Atonement. If one quantifies such things, *Yom Kippur* is the holiest day in the Jewish tradition, and *Kol Nidre*, named after the evening's major prayer, is a beautiful and moving service even the least observant Jew will usually attend. The music touches one's heart, allowing an opening to the Holy Day's twenty-five-hour fast dedicated to seek forgiveness and atonement for personal sins and those of the community.

I told Deloris the service was coming up and asked if she wanted to go. In previous years she had loved the ethereal music, the emotional release, the sense of belonging to something larger than herself. Now, I had no idea if the service had any meaning for her or how she would respond to my question. Animation suffused her face. "Yes, absolutely," she said.

I knew there would be procedural and logistic hurdles to overcome to get Deloris to this service, and I knew I would do whatever was necessary to make it happen.

The doctor approved the outing. Her nurses enthusiastically helped Deloris change from her usual attire of sweat pants and a fleece top into Temple-worthy clothes.

I would not soon forget the feeling I experienced walking into Temple that day, pushing Deloris's wheelchair. Happier than I had been in weeks, I felt truly blessed that Deloris was here with me only weeks after her stroke. Although I had hoped and dreamed it could happen, I don't think I really believed I would be entering the Temple with her, maybe ever again. Even though I knew only part of her was actually present, it was enough . . . for the moment.

We sat in the back of the sanctuary. Friends were excited to see Deloris. They came over, reintroduced themselves, and gave her a hug. Deloris seemed a bit overwhelmed, even nonplussed at the attention. She kept asking, "Why do these people care? Why are they happy to see me?" Often she prefaced these questions by asking, "Who was that?" She was, however, clearly warmed by this outpouring of love. I felt embraced and held in the arms of a loving and caring community, a feeling I found nourishing, if not essential, for my journey.

Deloris remained alert and awake throughout the several hour service, involved in her own prayers. She read our synagogue's little prayer book all the way through about three times, an unsurprising example of her obsessive behavioral characteristics. She actively participated in the communal readings and songs. She listened to the rabbi, sometimes asking me to repeat words she did not hear; she laughed at appropriate places and was solemn at others. She seemed to be as present as she was able. And she sang—it was the first time I remember her singing since her stroke. Before she was hospitalized, Deloris had sung all the time; she has a lovely singing voice. And while the quality had diminished a bit as a result of her condition, her voice was sweet music to my ears.

Back at the nursing facility later that night, Deloris reverted to her I'm-not-going-to-do-it-and-I-don't-have-to persona. I pleaded with her to change into pajamas and get into bed, and she said, "I am. I am just not doing it as fast as you would like." This refrain would become all too familiar in coming months and years.

I implored. I coaxed. Then my concern for catching a ferry overrode both the emotional serenity generated by the earlier religious experience and my understanding of what Deloris was capable of doing, and I became impatient. I became demanding. I spoke in absolutes.

"You have to change into your jammies. You have to go to bed now. No, you can't stay up." I forgot Deloris never responded positively to demands. Who among us does?

Finally, the negotiator in me stepped forward. I said, "If you do this for me, I have a treat for you." It was bribery, an approach familiar to parents of young children. Chocolate and a kiss can—and at this point did—work wonders. I was soon off in a frantic, and successful, dash to the ferry.

The next day Deloris was quiet and tired. The nursing staff said that she had been awake far into the night, much to the dismay of her new roommate. The excitement of being among so many friends, the thrill of the excursion, the emotional impact of the service, and perhaps some remembrance of earlier times in the same location, hearing the same music, reciting the same prayers tapped into an energy that precluded sleep.

"Did you enjoy last night?" I asked.

"What did we do?"

"Don't you remember?"

"No."

"We went to *Kol Nidre* services." "Sure, I remember. I was surprised I didn't see any friends there. I wonder why they weren't there."

"You don't remember seeing Stephen and Sheila?" I asked.

"Oh, yes. We saw them."

"What about Roger?

Do you remember seeing him? Or Ted?"

"Sure. I saw them." This exchange continued through the names of several other people, all of whom Deloris remembered seeing, but only after I mentioned their names. I attempted to absorb this reaction without understanding how to process it.

What was most compelling for me was what had happened that night once we returned to Deloris's room. In that place and time, Deloris had again become my teacher. Like many people, Deloris will not do something because someone tells her she has to. Her usual response is quite the opposite. Even with her brain functioning at less than optimal capacity, she still wanted a rationale she could process in her own way to determine whether my reason for her to act as I desired was sufficient reason for her to do it. Deloris wanted to be independent, her own person, a desire I wholeheartedly supported. At least in theory.

In her invalid condition, she had few opportunities to demonstrate any individuality or independence, other than saying no in the manner of a recalcitrant two-year-old. I did not believe Deloris was being intentionally stubborn. Nor did I think she was aware of the lessons she was teaching me. She was merely being herself, acting in the only way she knew how. I had to remember she was my wife, the woman I loved and shared my life with, and so deserved to be treated with more dignity, more sensitivity, more patience. I wondered how much more time and how many more incidents it would take for me to learn this lesson.

In the Still of the Night

It was difficult to maintain the calm, accepting demeanor with which I attempted to go through my days once I got to the still of late night, when the house was dark and silent. Faced with yet another night alone in bed, my mind replayed the day's events and my conversations and interactions with Deloris. I didn't focus on what I'd seen and felt or even what we'd talked about. At night I thought about what I'd lost.

I visualized Deloris sitting in a wheelchair in front of the nurses' station outside her room, obsessively reading and rereading words that did not penetrate her mind. I saw her failure to realize she didn't understand what she was reading. I heard her start sentences, but unable to remember what she wanted to say, let them trail off. I felt the emptiness beneath her exterior, the absence of energy, the void where there used to be ideas and passions, a sense of the absurd and of the divine. Her voice was similar, her touch somewhat the same, her joking an indistinct echo of what it once had been.

While I encountered these mental images, Deloris lay in a hospital bed thirty-five miles away, locked in neurological isolation where, blessedly, she seemed to feel little pain and only occasional anxiety. At mealtime, she ate with compulsion, licking every drop of artificially flavored ice cream, drinking pedestrian decaf coffee with non-dairy creamer, relishing canned vegetables and unidentifiable meat dishes. She enthusiastically devoured food that in times past would not have entered her journalistic food-critic mouth. This alone indicated to me how sick she was. She wrote, but the sentences made little sense. Her words and questions might have had surface meaning, but in context they were gibberish. She often did not know where she was, or why.

One day she was upset because she couldn't remember the name of Lydia's sister. Lydia, you may recall, is our cat. "Lydia doesn't have a sister," I said, "only a brother, Carlyle, who is no longer with us."

"Yes, she does," Deloris said. "We have three cats, Carlyle, Lydia, and one other, who is their sister. I just can't remember the other cat's name."

As we talked, I remembered that years ago we'd had a white cat living with us for about four days. This was a stray our neighbor in Seattle had asked us to care for. "Are you thinking about Bullion?" I asked. Neither Lydia nor Carlyle had liked Bullion. I'm not sure we did either. Several days after we spent about two hundred dollars in vet bills on this cat (yes, the cat was named for the cost of the vet bill, not his silver color.) Bullion had peed on the carpet one time too many, and we gave him (her? I don't remember) back to the neighbor.

"That's her name. I remember now." This conversation seemed to have been triggered by Deloris's flannel pajama pants, patterned with pictures of white cats. She associated these with the cat in history whose name she could not recall.

It wasn't my idea of a fruitful mental pursuit.

At other times Deloris wasn't sure where she was. She couldn't understand, for instance, why the cat wouldn't come when called, a concern I thought was especially odd since Lydia had never responded when beckoned. But I didn't mention that. I focused on the more obvious reason. "I think it's because Lydia is at home on Spyglass Drive, and you are in the hospital in Everett."

"I don't think so." Deloris was insistent.

"Sorry, it's true. Look around. Does this look like our house?"

"No. I guess you're right." At this Deloris became contrite and gave me a little window into her experience. "It's so hard to remember all this. I forget sometimes. I don't think my brain is functioning that well."

She was trying to make sense of her surroundings, a puzzle that confused her again and again.

One day, our friend Fredericka asked Deloris to describe what she felt like being sick.

"It reminds me of being in Nepal," she said. "There's a grayness to life. People all around me are sick and dying."

That certainly had been true of the areas near the temples in Nepal where we encountered lepers and other desperately ill beggars. It had also been true near the funeral pyres. Mostly, however, the Nepalese we met when we visited there were healthy, smiling, seemingly happy people.

I found the image fascinating. In the hospital and the rehab facility, Deloris was around very sick people, although they weren't necessarily dying. Perhaps this was how her subconscious was learning to deal with physical or mental deficits. I didn't totally agree with Deloris's description of Nepal. We both loved the country and the people we met there. I felt the analogy to her present condition was a stretch, but it was not my description that mattered. Deloris was describing her feelings, and the creativity of the analogy, however accurate, was undeniable. It was very Deloris-like, even in its being somewhat of a non sequitur. I was attracted to both aspects.

Unfortunately, my wife was not always able to be creative in her difficulties. One day when I got to Deloris's room, she had an Everett phone book open on her table. She was frustrated not to find my number in it. I tried to explain that we didn't live in Everett so the number wouldn't be there. I wrote my cell number and our home phone number in black numbers and pinned it on the bulletin board across from her bed. This relieved her anxiety. Knowing where to find it and feeling she could connect with me whenever she wished to made her feel better.

I, however, became even more concerned. Deloris's inability to negotiate even this simple task on her own left me with a sense of profound unease. I knew she had made incredible progress since being hospitalized. I understood we were poised at the beginning of a long process in which she would continue to improve, would plateau a number of times, and even regress at times. Hopefully, her arc would continue heading upward. Though I was prepared for this journey intellectually, I doubted I would ever feel ready emotionally. At night, alone in bed, I cried for my loss. Tears bathed my mental images of Deloris's complacent, irrational self; they washed visions of her struggling to stand up, attempting—and failing—to exert independence. Even in the bathroom she needed help.

In these melancholy hours, the thought of our walking on the beach, going to movies, traveling, even sharing an evening with friends, seemed so remote it was mental self-flagellation to consider them. When I thought how those simple actions were beyond her present ability, the sadness generated by that perception of loss was excruciating.

The loss of words, her inability to complete thoughts, was especially worrying. This was not a language deficiency, since Deloris had a large and varied vocabulary. Rather it was the result of aphasia, a cognitive condition in which one cannot access, or does not remember, the desired word. Deloris had the language; she could not reach the place where it was stored. If the mind was a perfect library, as a friend had once described it, then some of Deloris's stacks were presently inaccessible because of obstacles. The pathways needed to be reformed.

That reformation was a major objective of her therapy. It was similar to teaching a young child to think and solve problems. Except Deloris was an adult, not a small child. I couldn't shake the feeling that adults were not supposed to have to go through this process. Again.

I had always gone to bed late at night. I knew being awake at 1:30 or 2:00 a.m. was not the healthiest idea. However, it was one way I coped with the situation I found myself in. Crying was another. Allowing my pain to surface however it chose felt therapeutic. The anguish was certainly real. I felt it more often and in greater intensity than I allowed myself to admit.

I knew it did no good to stay in that dark place. I helped neither Deloris nor myself by living in a painful fantasy of future incompetence, especially since there was no reason to believe it was the only, or even the most expected, probability. The present reality was hard enough, despite being in many ways positive.

Deloris had improved, and more progress was expected. She was happy, or at least peaceful. She lived in the present, something I strived to achieve in my spiritual practice. Of course, her present reality was not always the shared one. That was a problem, but only to me, not to her. Many nights, I had to wipe away the tears before I could try to sleep.

I Wanted Some Chocolate

Her bed was empty, the sheets and blanket tucked tightly under the mattress, ready for a new resident. Institutional green paint was all too visible on now bare walls. The pictures of family and friends, the cards that yesterday covered the surface had disappeared. The flowers that lined her windowsill yesterday were gone.

I walked to the nurses' station with a puzzled look on my face. The duty nurse, seeing me, smiled and said, "We had to move her. She's now in room 414 across the hall from us."

"Why?"

"She went missing for about twenty minutes late yesterday afternoon. Someone found her on the first floor, standing in front of the gift shop. So, we moved her to the room across from us where we can keep a closer watch on her."

"Well, she never was one to miss a retail opportunity." The familiar quip barely masked my concern. How was Deloris able to leave a secure ward, walk all the way down the hall, get into an elevator, exit four floors later, and walk to the gift shop with no hospital personnel seeing her or thinking to ask what she was doing? Her plastic identification bracelet, if nothing else, clearly indicated she was a patient, even though she wore her own clothes.

"Apparently, she memorized the key code when the physical therapist took her for a walk." The nurse seemed impressed with my wife's ingenuity and struggle to maintain some independence even as she was concerned for Dee's safety. So was I. The stroke had disrupted Deloris's brain functions and cognitive abilities. Yet, the neurological damage she had suffered did not prevent her from remembering the six-number sequence necessary to open the double doors separating the rehabilitation unit from the more publicly accessible parts of the hospital. More likely, she memorized hand and finger positions. I doubted she could tell me the sequence, as I was sure it was stored somewhere below her conscious level. However she managed it, the feat was as impressive as it was a matter of concern.

I laughed, thanked the nurse, and went across the hall to find my wife.

Her new room was a mirror image of her old one. A hospital bed and side table dominated the space, along with an easy chair. The wall across from the bed contained a small, chest-high dresser and a washbasin topped by a mirror. A door across from the bed opened into a small closet. A television set hung from the ceiling. All of Deloris's flowers, cards, and pictures had been moved into this room and placed in position. A large plastic water cup, topped by a cap with a plastic flexible straw sticking out, sat on the table next to her. Deloris lay in bed, half-gazing at the daytime game show filling the television screen.

"Hi, hon," I said.

She turned slowly in the direction of my voice. When she recognized me, light and animation enlivened her face. "Hello, love." The words struggled to leave her mouth and warmed my heart as I heard them.

"Heard you had a bit of an adventure yesterday."

Deloris looked blank, unable to process my statement.

"The nurse said you left the floor and went down to the gift store." Remembrance filled her face. "Why'd you do that?"

"I wanted some chocolate." The explanation seemed logical to her. She wanted chocolate and went to where she thought she might find it. We had taken an excursion to the gift shop earlier, so both the path to the shop and perhaps the memory of its contents were mentally accessible. The fact she had no money and the shop was closed had not entered her mind. Rather, there was only desire that enabled her to stand, walk out of her room, down the hall, open a locked door, proceed to an elevator, figure out what floor she wanted, and get to her destination. All by herself. This from a woman who needed assistance to take the several steps from her bed to the bathroom. The accomplishment was impressive—and more than a bit scary.

"You have chocolate on the counter, and the drawer next to your bed is filled with it. There is probably some in your pocket, and most assuredly a piece or two on the window sill." Chocolate had always been a favorite of Dee's but recently it had achieved an almost obsessive stature in her life. Little else gave her equivalent pleasure. "Why did you want more?" I asked.

"Really? I have chocolate here?" She was incredulous. "I don't think so. Where is it?"

I opened the drawer in her bedside table and showed her. She smiled at the trove within her reach. She selected a piece, and, putting it in her mouth, she leaned back on her pillow, content.

STOP!

The hand-lettered sign hanging on the barrier across the door to Deloris's room contained only a single word: STOP! An electric eye about eight inches from the floor triggered an alarm whenever anyone crossed the threshold. Apparently, moving Deloris within eyesight of the nurses' station was not enough.

"What's all this about?" I asked the duty nurse.

She explained that Deloris had demonstrated increased mobility in her new room and this had encouraged the nurses to give her the run of the place. Taking full advantage of this new freedom, Deloris had wandered all over the floor, going in and out of other patients' rooms. "Yesterday we found her on the floor in some else's bathroom," the nurse said. Apparently, having finished her business and trying to stand, Deloris had fallen. She'd hurt her face, but it was nothing serious, "this time," the nurse added.

"We are encouraged by her increased mobility and sense of balance," she said. "Even a week ago, she wouldn't have been capable of roaming like this. But she doesn't realize how dangerous this is for her. And she had no idea she was in someone else's room. She thought it was her own room."

The nurses decided to use technology to minimize the danger of Deloris's hurting herself, giving her full freedom to move around within the confines of her room and having her ask permission whenever she wants to leave the room.

"How's that working out?" I asked.

"Could be better," the nurse said with a laugh.

"Last night we found her on the floor. She was on her back; one leg was sticking out of the door under the electric eye beam." Either she was practicing for a limbo contest or she was trying to figure out how to get out of the room by crawling under the beam. The attempt reminded me of the some years before when I had a goat who would stand in front of the electric fence and time the surges. At least that was what she appeared to be doing. Then, in between the current surges, she would dash through the fence in order to eat the grass on the other side. That there was no difference in the quality of the food was unimportant; the grass is always greener. "Impressive," I said, my pride at Deloris's agility and determination mixed in equal proportion with apprehension for her safety. The nurse agreed. That these antics were also potentially dangerous and a major inconvenience for the nursing staff went unspoken but was mutually understood.

The nurse showed me how to turn off the electric eye. I removed the spring-loaded barrier and entered Deloris's room. She was sitting in a chair watching TV. Happy to see me, she smiled broadly and held up her face for a kiss. Naturally, I obliged.

"How are you feeling?" I asked.

"Okay."

"Whatcha been doing since I saw you yesterday? Anything exciting going on?"

"Nothing much."

"Do you know why there is a barrier across the door to your room? Or how you got that bruise over your right eye?"

"I don't have a bruise. Do I really? What barrier?"

I was not surprised at her lack of awareness of the changes in the entryway or her not remembering having fallen. It was typical of the way Deloris's mind was working, or not working, depending on one's point of view.

I sat in the other chair and we talked some more until her recreational therapist came in for her scheduled appointment. I had met the therapist several days before when we had talked about Deloris's reading habit. "When I came into her room yesterday," the therapist said to me, "Deloris was reading a book about flower arranging. She probably got it from the library collection we have in the dining room."

I explained that Deloris had studied ikebana, Japanese flower arranging, for a number of years and was a certified trained instructor.

Later, I asked Deloris about the book since I didn't see it in her room.

"I took it back to the dining room." she said. "It really wasn't about flower arranging. It just had pictures of flowers in it. The therapist is such a nice lady I didn't want to embarrass her by saying anything. So, I just agreed with her."

I smiled. The response and the refusal to embarrass another was pure Deloris.

* * *

Between visits, I was preparing, physically and emotionally, for my wife's return home, tentatively scheduled to take place the end of October, a week away. The reality of my becoming a full-time caregiver for an invalid wife was beginning to sink in. The first thing I had to do was make sure the house was safe for her return.

We knew the two-story house in which we lived might eventually become impractical. We had looked for months to find a house we liked in which we could live on one floor. Deloris fell in love with our present house the first time she saw it. Although I was less taken with it, I acquiesced to its purchase after we agreed we would sell it if one of us became incapable of climbing the stairs to our second floor bedroom. The layout of the house and the size of the rooms made living on the main floor impractical.

I spent hours on the Internet researching ideas to make the house safer and more convenient for Deloris. Several friends, including an architect and a neurology-trained nurse, walked through the house with me, making further suggestions. Some of the suggested modifications were both easy and obvious. When Deloris's aunt was living with us, we had installed a downstairs shower with grab bars and added grab bars in the bathroom she used. I now installed more grab bars in both upstairs bathrooms and removed rugs that might be a slipping hazard. Other suggestions, such as putting a master bedroom and bath on the main floor, were more difficult and more expensive. Still other modifications, like an elevator, however appropriate, were nearly impossible, given the house's floor plan.

In the years we had lived in this house, I had grown very fond of it and its location. While I knew it was just a house, during the weeks Deloris was in the hospital, it had become my sanctuary, a place of peace and serenity. I also thought Deloris's familiarity with it might be useful, especially in the early stages of her at-home rehabilitation. She needed these types of cognitive clues to trigger appropriate mental responses. Not only was I reluctant to make major decisions; in truth, I didn't have the energy for it. What was important now was getting Deloris home and making the house safe and ready for her.

By focusing on mundane, practical matters, I was able to push aside the emotions roiling below the surface. The difficulties I experienced in my daily commutes to the hospital were considerably easier than the issues I would be faced with when Deloris was at home. While she was in hospital, I had no responsibilities for her care. Other people made sure she was fed, clothed, monitored, and medicated. Therapists worked with her to increase her mental, physical, and social capabilities. I was free to come and go as I pleased, able to miss days if I needed or wanted to do something else. My life revolved around her condition and hospitalization, but only in a general, emotional sense and not the everyday, all the time, "it's all up to me" situation we were about to enter. Without fully realizing the deeper, underlying reasons, I focused on the routine: the immediate, practical necessities of getting the house ready for Deloris's return. This approach, one I would return to numerous times in subsequent months and years, allowed me to take care of business and maintain some emotional stability.

While I looked forward to having Deloris home, I recognized it would have a major impact on my life. I had no way of knowing the exact nature of these changes, nor did I dwell on this unknown future. What I did know is that I would learn the lessons I needed to learn. I would do whatever needed to be done. I would learn to float.

Last Days in Hospital

I spent an afternoon shadowing the therapists in what was called "family training." With the physical therapist (PT) at her side, Deloris climbed up and down stairs with and without the use of a handrail. She practiced walking on a variety of surfaces from a smooth interior floor to a rough and uneven gravel driveway. She practiced getting in and out of the car. She did well on all of it, although she didn't pay close attention to where she was going, and she wasn't aware of the possibility of oncoming traffic. Luckily, we live on a quiet street.

The PT was not only helping Deloris learn these basic skills, she was also teaching me the appropriate ways to be of assistance. Deloris retook a balance test, which she had first attempted two weeks earlier. Her score went from thirty-six to forty-nine, a substantial increase.

She still had some balance problems but was getting better. Safety and awareness clearly remained concerns.

Our next stop was the kitchen where her occupational therapists (OTs) asked Deloris to cook an egg and make some tea. At first Deloris wanted a kettle to make a pot of tea but agreed with the OT's request to use the microwave and make a single cup. This was better practice for how we did things at home.

Deloris did a good job of scrambling an egg for me, making sure to use garlic salt, remembering my love of garlic. When I commented on the amount of garlic salt she was using, Deloris reminded me how much I like garlic and said she was making the egg for me, causing me to smile at her desire to please. It took her a long time to complete the task, requiring lots of verbal cues and refocusing from the OTs. It was the first time in two months Deloris had been in a kitchen, and this particular kitchen was unfamiliar. She seemed competent, if not totally comfortable. Both the egg and the tea were tasty and well done.

Her speech therapist worked with her on verbal and aural comprehension by having her read a paragraph and answer questions. She did okay. She reread the paragraph to find the answers to those questions she couldn't answer from memory. She showed improved problem solving skills. Her short-term memory in other aspects was not so good. Deloris was still confabulating, although not as creatively as before. On balance, I think that was actually good news.

The prospect of Deloris being home had become a stressor in my life. On my last night alone, I lay in bed, mixed thoughts rolling around my mind. I had done all the initial changes to de-clutter the house and get it ready for her. I moved furniture, removing pieces I thought might be obstacles. I repositioned our bed so it would be easier for her to get in and out of it. The rugs had been taken up, exposing hardwood floors that posed less danger for slipping. I attached labels to all the kitchen drawers and cabinet doors, identifying their contents. While the house was as ready as I knew how to make it, I wasn't sure I was personally ready.

October 30, 2005

Tomorrow's the day! Deloris is ready. She's talking about being home and being bored.

Today, the physical therapist took her on two field trips — the first to the gift shop to see if Deloris could find things that she wanted. That was successful, although no purchases were made. A later trip to Safeway was different. Many more people, many more items, much more stimulation. Deloris was easily distracted and tired after a short while. She wanted to buy some sort of bag to carry things in; she found what she wanted and the PT gave her the money to pay for it. Rather than going through the line to the cashier, she put the money into the bag, folded the bag up, and put it back on the shelf. She then walked away, becoming distracted by something else. Clearly something I need to be aware of when we go to the store.

My brother, Mark, is planning on visiting at the end of the week. Always good to see him, and it will be nice to have some help and company for a few days. In the meantime, I need to post signs on all the drawers and cabinets to let Deloris know what is there. Visual cues are important for her. I should also finish cleaning the house. We moved furniture today, clearing space, especially in the bedroom. Still some more space to clear.

I am excited about Deloris being home and, of course, somewhat apprehensive about making sure that she is safe, and I have some semblance of a life other than as a caregiver. It will be great not having to commute to Everett every day and feeling somewhat guilty when I leave to come home, with Deloris alone in her room. I know there is no right way to do this, and I can only be a help to Dee if I am healthy and true to myself. This will be easier if I don't have to commute and feel guilty about leaving. And, for those of you on the Island, you can come visit in much more comfortable surroundings than a hospital room.

So, tomorrow, a new leg of the journey, a new phase of our existence, individual and collective, begins. Is there some significance that it is also Halloween?

Allan

CHAPTER SIX
MOORING, AT LAST

Home Again, Home Again

THE BACK OF the Honda was loaded with clothes, books, magazines, a radio, and chocolates. Flowers and plants were tucked into any remaining space, even after we left bouquets at the nurses' stations. Deloris had been discharged, and we were headed home, back to Whidbey Island. I was excited and more than a little apprehensive about what the future would bring. Her flat affect made it difficult for me to determine Deloris's emotions, although I assumed she was happy about going home. Hopefully, the familiarity of home would trigger memories and help synapses to reconnect.

Re-entry began calmly enough. Friends brought over dinner and a couple of bottles of nice wine. Midway through the meal, Deloris attempted to stand up. "I want to get my black cape, the one with the purple silk lining," she declared. "Tonight's Halloween and I want to be ready."

"We've never had trick-or-treaters in all the years we've lived in this house," I said, amazed she knew what day it was.

"I want to be ready just in case."

"Okay. I think the cape is in the closet upstairs." I helped her to stand. We went up the fourteen stairs to our second floor bedroom. Unfortunately, we were unable to find the cape. When she saw the bed, Deloris wanted to lie down. The excitement of the day had worn her out.

After getting her comfortable in bed, I returned to our guests, only to jump up and climb the stairs every ten or fifteen minutes. I didn't trust Deloris would or could call me if she needed something. I feared she might attempt to come down the stairs by herself. And while she would probably be able to handle the stairs perfectly, I knew I couldn't assume that.

"I'm fine," she said each time I asked. "What's all the fuss about?" I wished I knew how to explain it to her. Clearly, it would take me time to adjust to having Deloris home-and dependent on me.

It felt good to have her home, and I was relieved not to have a daily commute to the hospital. I was also gratified by her progress since the stroke. Deloris is extremely intelligent with an active and inquisitive mind, so I couldn't begin to guess how much more progress she might make. Jill Bolte Taylor, an academic neuro-anatomist, in her book My Stroke of Insight, said it took her eight years to achieve an almost complete recovery from the massive left hemispheric stroke she suffered. At the same time, I knew most stroke victims experience more progress during the first three to six months than at any other time. It was important for me to remain positive and hopeful-and to remember that each person's situation is unique. Deloris wasn't Jill Bolte Taylor and she wasn't most stroke victims; she was her own person. On the other hand, I couldn't help but notice that while she had regained a great deal, she still had significant deficits from her pre-stroke abilities and personality.

When she was lucid, Deloris seemed normal. Unless you'd had a recent exchange with her, it would be difficult for you to know anything was awry. When she was confabulating or off on one of her flights of fancy, her conversation still made sense, at least on the surface. You would have to have a history with Deloris, some background about her, to make an accurate evaluation. Unfortunately, since I had the background experience, I found her continued confabulation frustrating and, at times, heart-wrenching. Her stories were vivid reminders to me that she was not well. My heart kept trying to convince me she was better than my mind knew she was.

Deloris wanted to improve, and she had the intellectual capacity to do so. Whether or not she had the will to do what was necessary to establish the mental and neurological workarounds to compensate for all those missing neural connections remained an unknown. How that would happen, how long it would take, and if it would happen, were yet to be seen.

That first night at home, what mattered to me most was that I would get to sleep with my wife in our own bed for the first time in two months.

I wish I could say that first night home was an unqualified success. It wasn't. About 2:30 a.m. Deloris awoke, took a trip to the bathroom, and had trouble falling back asleep. Her restless movements kept me awake as I hovered over her like a mother hen. We finally drifted back to sleep only to redo the dance at about 4:00 a.m. This time it was harder to get back to sleep, although ultimately we were successful, waking for the day about 7:45.

Most of that first full day at home was spent in routine matters. We ran errands and Deloris spent a great deal of time in the bathroom, which she seemed to have converted into a reading room. Everything was all right until after dinner, when our cat Lydia made an appearance. As she moved to pet Lydia, Deloris fell, banging against a chair. She hurt her knee, which made it difficult for her to stand and walk. Climbing the stairs to the bedroom proved painful; Deloris had to crawl up the last few stairs on hands and knees. She collapsed, out of breath, at the top. After regaining her breath, she stood and made it into bed, relieved and exhausted.

We were both shaken by the fall. Not only was Deloris in pain, but the fall underscored that she was not as physically able as we both had considered her to be. The limitations of her capacities were becoming real to her in a way they had not been before. That was probably a benefit.

I had been lulled a bit by how well she seemed to be doing in her therapy. I was convinced she would regain her old abilities through a combination of her own hard work and my mental determination that she get better. That she was not as functional as I'd believed was something I'd never considered. Nor had I thought about the potential harm that might result from my letting down my guard even for a minute. The realization of how easily Deloris could hurt herself shocked and frightened me. Her fall made me see how attentive I would have to be.

Sleeping was clearly going to be a challenge now. My habit of going to bed after midnight had to change. The experiences of Deloris's first night at home made it apparent I was going to be awakened several times during the night. Tension, irritability, mood swings, and other symptoms of sleep deprivation commonly experienced by the parents of newborn children, might soon begin to manifest in me.

Our lives and relationship had changed dramatically. I could not yet begin to imagine the extent of changes still to come. It was going to be a day-to-day journey. At the time I knew I had to avoid getting frustrated at slow progress and at the incapacities that would continue to limit Deloris's independence-not to mention the behaviors she either couldn't control or employed in order to carve out some small degree of freedom and independence.

Even with these difficulties, adjustments, and unknowns, I was happy to have her home.

A Major Step Forward

For more than two decades, Deloris had been Seattle's foremost art critic and I knew sooner or later she would be asked to reassume her art critic persona. So, I wasn't surprised when several weeks after her return home, she received a request for an interview call from a freelance journalist working on a piece on Northwest Art for The New York Times.

"You need to know," I told him, "my wife has recently suffered a stroke. I am not sure how much she is able to remember and relate as she has trouble staying in the collective reality." I hoped being honest about her condition could dissuade him, as I was not sure the interview was a good idea.

"I had heard about that, and I'm really sorry," he said. "I hope she's doing better." He added, "I'd still like to talk with her."

Deloris wanted to do the interview, so I resumed my role as her driver and personal assistant. The meeting was scheduled for the Museum of Northwest Art in LaConner, Washington, a ninety-minute drive from our house. An exhibit of some of the work described in Deloris's book on Northwest art, Iridescent Light, was on display at the museum, providing an appropriate backdrop for the interview.

As was becoming all too normal, I had not allowed enough time for Deloris to get up, dressed, and have breakfast. I nagged her in an almost abusive manner to move faster than she was willing or perhaps able to do. Finally on our way, we listened to a book on tape in the car, both because it was our habit and also so we did not have to talk to each other. The conversation might not have been very pleasant, given the tension between Deloris and me, and how outraged I was with myself for the way I had been acting.

We were late getting to LaConner, a fact that seemed to concern only me. The journalist greeted Deloris as if keeping him waiting for almost a half-hour was a normal occurrence. Maybe it was, or maybe he was more invested in getting the interview than we were in giving it. Whatever the reason, I was relieved by his reaction.

We sat on a bench surrounded by paintings by artists featured in Deloris's book. She faced the interviewer, while I sat behind her, giving them some visual privacy, yet ready to intervene if I thought Deloris needed care or was becoming incoherent. I needn't have worried. From the first question, Deloris transformed into the professional art critic and author.

Engaged in, and by, a subject she knew well, Deloris was no longer the less-than-competent stroke victim. Eyes alert and focused with an intensity I had not seen since her stroke, she engaged with the interviewer. Her answers were insightful, full of facts, critical observations, and equal in quality to what she was used to giving before her stroke. She basked in the compliments the freelancer gave her on the quality of her book and her knowledge of and insight into Northwest art. I was amazed at how easily Deloris was able to become a professional again, to speak knowledgeably and with clarity about relatively esoteric theories and concepts.

It was another example for me of the duality that existed in my wife's mind. Some parts of her brain, especially those dealing with long-term memory and professional expertise, seemed easily accessed; other areas, such as those used in decision-making, remained blocked or nonfunctioning. I considered the possibility that having opportunities to be her old self might well be a therapeutic key to her recovery.

I also wondered as well if there might not be cognitive and neurological portals Deloris could access that had not been available before her stroke. As previously dormant parts of her brain became available for rewiring the pathways necessary for her to function, did memories of the past months take her to new levels of awareness? Might what we call deficits actually enable Deloris to achieve a level of mindfulness and consciousness not otherwise available? Jill Bolte Taylor described how her own stroke caused her to lose total functioning of her left-brain and, at the same time, activated the right side of her brain, opening her to an almost spiritual sense of interdependence and universal connection. Deloris's stroke, on the right side of her brain, did not have the same devastating physical and cognitive consequences as did Taylor's. Nonetheless, I was curious to see what, if any, emotional and attitudinal changes might be triggered by the physiological and neurological damage Deloris suffered.

When I awoke each morning, I had difficulty accepting I had no answers to these big questions. At a more immediate level, I was even unsure how to deal with the mundane issues Deloris's condition brought up. I became increasingly stressed, in large part, I think, because I had been going nonstop for the more than two months since her stroke. I could not leave her alone and was unwilling to leave her with a non-family caregiver.

While not necessarily rational, my fears were real to me. If I left her alone and something happened to her, I felt I would, at a minimum, be in therapy about it for the rest of my life. I kept thinking in terms of worst-case scenarios: Deloris, alone in the house, having suffered another stroke, unaware of the need to call 911, and my arriving home too late to prevent serious and permanent damage from occurring.

Of course, this could just as easily have occurred at any time in our pre-stroke past, when we thought nothing of being apart. We had our separate friends with whom we spent time; we both had business trips that took us out of town for days at a time. While we cherished our time together, our time apart nourished us, as did the freedom of expression and action we gave each other. This trust and mutual respect was part of the foundation of our relationship. Even in the present situation, where such freedom and extended separation was not possible, my focusing on worst-case scenarios was a recipe for craziness. I had to learn to trust, to begin to let go of the reins, to make this more of a partnership. I wanted to give Deloris some freedom. I needed to trust she would be able to take care of herself and use the phone if there was a problem. It wasn't going to be easy for me, but I knew I had to try.

"What do you think about staying in the house by yourself for maybe an hour every once in a while?" I asked her one day. "I could really use some time for myself."

"Sure. You could use the break and I can take care of myself. Just leave me the car keys."

"Yeah, like that's going to happen." Deloris's driving was another issue entirely. I brought her back to the subject at hand. "I'm sure you'll be okay for thirty minutes or so. Any longer would make me uncomfortable." Then I explained why. "If something happened to you while I was away, I could never forgive myself. Maybe I'll find some friends or hire some professional help to stay with you for longer stretches."

Deloris seemed to understand my concerns and fears; hopefully she heard the love that lay below my comments. She said, "You used to travel a lot for school. You liked it and I think you should keep going to Phoenix since it makes you feel good. You deserve it." She thought for a moment. "My sisters, or my daughter, could come and stay with me. I could even stay by myself."

We continued to brainstorm solutions to give me time for myself and the ability to accept out-of-town teaching assignments. The work would give us some additional income as well as providing me a different energy focus.

That we could discuss these issues and attempt to collaborate on solutions felt like a major step forward toward returning to some sense of normalcy-always the goal.

Developing a New Normal

The first time she got out of bed without help after returning home, Deloris didn't remember falling, even though the event was indelibly etched in my mind. So she had to do it all over again the next day. She got up from a nap, slipped, and fell, landing on her back. She was on the floor before I heard any movement. Luckily, the only harm was to her pride. Some aids to help her be more stable when she walked around the house seemed to be needed. I obtained a couple of canes, a walker, and borrowed a wheelchair for Deloris to use. After reminding her a number of times to "get your cane," or asking "where's your walker?" I suggested she name them. She did: Her primary cane became known as Raisin and her walker Johnny. The secondary cane she called Michael. The wheelchair was never named. We returned it after about a year, because her reliance on its use became detrimental to her progress. Since she was not walking as much as she could, and should have, she was losing muscle tone and energy. Raisin cane gave her some additional stability when she walked. If we were going a long distance, using Johnny walker provided increased assistance and comfort, as it had a seat on which Deloris could rest when she tired.

Previously, we had discussed her calling for me if she wanted to get up when I wasn't in the room, but apparently she hadn't remembered the conversation. Either that, or she hadn't wanted to remember it. I couldn't blame her. I remembered how difficult it was for me to be dependent on others when I was on crutches for three months after running a lawn mower over my foot. It's hard being reliant on others when one has been independent most of one's life. Since it would be next to impossible to stop Deloris from doing what she wanted, all I could do was make the house as safe as possible and trust she would not hurt herself.

I found myself on the edge of almost constant frustration with the changes the stroke caused in my wife. Deloris still engaged in obsessive behavior; whether this was caused by the stroke was never established. She continued to spend a great deal of time reading the same magazine articles over and over. Whether any information registered with her was impossible to tell. She also started reading aloud anything she found interesting. While some of the magazine articles were entertaining, the Yellow Pages of the Whidbey Island phone book, the reading material of choice for one car ride, were less than engaging.

Deloris looked mature and I knew she was intelligent, but in dealing with her, I sometimes thought she was acting like a pre-school child. That she was using the vocabulary of a well-educated adult in her lapses only complicated matters. I knew her behavior was not a conscious decision, although at times it seemed as if she was acting this way on purpose. The stroke's impact on her brain had her processing information and interacting with the world in the only way she was able. The main adjustment to be made was my own. I had to figure out how to make the best of a situation I never would have chosen.

To help Deloris improve her memory and ability to process information, we started playing a game. Each day she chose three words she had to remember. Throughout the day, I would ask her to repeat the words. She usually remembered one or two but seldom all three. For instance, if the words were pumpkin, apricot, and turtle, she'd remember pumpkin and apricot, coming up with a story to help her memory. "When I was young, my father brought home a pumpkin so we could make a jack-o-lantern for Halloween. It was the same color as dried apricots."

"What's the third word?"

"I don't remember."

"What's the candy that is chocolate covered pecans with caramel?" I asked.

"Turtles," she said. "I wish I had some right now!" Chocolate, of course, always worked as a key to her remembering.

Deloris frequently spent time either in bed or downstairs, lying on Kay's old hospital bed, which we had placed in the living room by a window looking out onto the flowers, birds, and, often deer, in the front yard. Deloris referred to the spot as her "day bed" and spent time there reading her old journals. Hopefully, they provided some stimulation to her memory, filling in the holes.

She became frustrated with my use of we in referring to things that I would like her to do. I would say, "We need to take a shower." Or, "Let's stand on the count of three and walk to the table."

"Why are you saying we?" Deloris asked me one day.

"We're a team," I explained.

"No, we're not. I want to do this myself. I need to be independent and do things myself, and you aren't letting me."

"You're right. But I am really concerned that you might fall again. I can't let that happen."

"Not to worry," she said. "I can do this. Walking is no problem. I am not going to fall."

Her logic and perception of reality differed so greatly from mine it made me uneasy. I needed to develop some coping strategies that meshed with her logic and worldview. I would have to live in and work with her reality.

Deloris's grasp of our reality was sketchy at best. When operating in her own reality, she was highly functional and creative. She described several ideas for new writing projects-a sequel to Ninety-Day Night, the vampire novel she was working on before the stroke; Saint Dave, a fictionalized story of her younger brother; a short story about aliens who come to earth and wind up as patients in a hospital emergency room-all highly creative ideas. It was impossible to know if she would remember these plans for more than a day much less actualize any of them. I told myself to be happy her mind functioned well enough to allow a creative flash.

Deloris wanted more than that. She experienced frustration at not being able to do things she thought needed to be done. One day when she was becoming upset about this, I asked her, "What is on your list that you think needs to be done but hasn't been?"

She was silent for a few minutes, obviously searching in her mind for the answer. "I don't know," she finally said. "I can't remember."

"There's a time to do and a time to be," I explained. "Maybe this is your time to be. The only thing you have to do is heal. I can take care of the rest. Enjoy not having outside responsibilities. Explore what's happening to you internally. The outside world's not going anywhere. It'll still be here when you're ready for it. You'll have other to-do lists, and if they are anything like mine, they'll have the same things on them, whether or not you do them now."

"Okay," she said. "I really don't have the energy to do anything anyway, and I can't remember what needs to be done. So, I think I'll go lie down."

"Good idea," I said as I left the room. "Have a nice nap." Deloris slept a great deal, sometimes for hours at a time, seldom getting out of bed, except for bathroom trips and to eat. I worked on accepting these cycles, recognizing the healing value of sleep. I remained concerned for her safety and found myself going upstairs every couple of hours, looking in the bedroom, to be sure she was still breathing. While I knew this was overreaction, I couldn't help myself. Mixed in with the concern was the relief that she was comfortable. Besides her being asleep made life a little easier for me.

Whenever Deloris was awake, I found myself struggling to find the right balance between giving her independence and maintaining a sufficiently tight leash to feel sure she was safe. The struggle strained us both. While her improvement was obvious, it was less than she thought it was. Unfortunately, her physical progress was not matched by her decision-making ability. A lot of our arguments were about time-Deloris's being on time, getting something done in time, or taking too much time for something. When she did not act with the speed I felt a situation called for, I became frustrated and angry. Increasingly over time, I communicated my wishes-my demands - with Deloris in language and at a volume one should never use with a loved one. Deloris accused me of being a dictator. I wondered if she wasn't, for her part, contributing to the impasse by digging in her heels, metaphorically speaking, to claim some personal autonomy. That vexing thought was the crux of our problem, but I didn't realize it at the time. As we struggled, I felt terrible when I became demanding and angry. I hated the way the situation we were in was changing our relationship.

At least a part of our problem was resolved by time itself. As weeks progressed, each day brought Deloris a slight increase in ability and mobility. I began to give her more space and freedom, motivated in part by being tired of struggling when she resisted demands-which, I had to admit--I had made for my own convenience, not hers. I was also getting comfortable accepting that she could wander around the house without harming herself. While I worried I might lull myself into a false sense of security, I knew I could not be with my wife every second of the day. I had to trust my instincts, and I had to trust her.

She talked about writing again, but I sensed she felt some reluctance, perhaps fear, in the voiced desire. She carried her journals from room to room as she moved through the day, pen in hand. I was never sure if she was just reading the old journals or actually writing something; it really didn't matter. Like other things, the writing would come when she was ready.

We both read Still Here, Ram Dass's book on aging which he completed writing after suffering a stroke. I had admired Ram Dass's spiritual approach to life for many years and thought Deloris might find his latest book enjoyable and useful since it dealt with issues similar to hers. She spent a long while reading and rereading the book. Years later when I asked what she'd liked in the book, Deloris said his discussion of the spiritual dimensions of being healed from a stroke resonated with her. Her experience made her conscious of her own finite nature, and especially grateful for being alive. And, as a writer, Deloris said she was also taken by some of his imagery and phrasing. Both aspects of her involvement with the book resulted in lots of highlighting and underlining.

When she wasn't reading Ram Dass's book, she spent time on her computer reading Wikipedia entries on backgammon written in Spanish. I had no idea why, or any idea how much of it she comprehended. I knew she had some moderate fluency in the language, which she demonstrated both during our trips to Mexico and with the earlier exchange with the rehab therapist. Some major parts of Deloris's mind clearly worked; at the same time, she still confabulated a great deal. I found the combinations of fact and fiction that developed in her mind annoying at times, but mainly I was amused and entertained by them.

One day Deloris made her own sandwich for lunch, the first time she had been so motivated. The task involved handling a sharp knife, which worried me a bit. It went well. She also decided to take a shower and wash her hair, again without my help, as in the past. That, too, went well.

I felt we might be entering a new phase. Deloris was sure of it.

It Was a Nightmare but, Unfortunately, Not a Dream

Noise filtered into my consciousness, rousing me from sleep. It was the middle of January. The dark room gave little clue to the hour, since there are not many hours of daylight during a Pacific Northwest winter. I eventually realized the noise I heard was the front doorbell. In the middle of the night, someone at the door is never the bearer of good news.

When I turned on the entry light and peered through the glass, I was stunned. Deloris sat on the bench outside the front door, her face covered with blood! I opened the door, and the stranger ringing my doorbell wordlessly turned, walked back to his pickup truck, and drove away.

"My God. What happened?" Panic mixed with concern as I moved to where Deloris was sitting.

"I fell," she said. "When I woke up, I wanted to work the crossword puzzle, so I went out to the mailbox to get the newspaper. It was really dark, and I couldn't see very well. I was worried that I would fall off the side of the driveway." I didn't remind her that the driveway is flat. "I got out to the street and the paper wasn't there."

"That's 'cause it usually doesn't come until around seven. You were out there hours too early."

"I didn't know," she said. "Somehow I tripped and fell on my face. I couldn't get up. I sat there in the middle of the street for hours. It was really cold, wet, and dark. I was scared. When I heard a car coming up the hill, I waved my hands. This man saw me and stopped. I told him I was trying to get to my husband who lived in the house over here. He put me in his truck and drove here. I was scared And cold."

I shuddered, thinking of Deloris sitting in the middle of a darkened road, dressed in a dark coat, dark pants, hat, and gloves, appropriate clothes given the weather. No one driving up the hill quickly would have seen her. The truck must have been slow, because, as Deloris told me later, the driver didn't have his lights on.

I helped my wife to her feet and into the house. In the bathroom, I began to wash off the blood and inspected the damage. It was obvious her condition warranted a trip to the emergency room. I felt relieved she was lucid enough to explain what happened since she looked like a domestic violence victim. Funny, the thoughts that go through your mind in times of stress.

"Why did you do that? You could have been seriously hurt or even killed." I knew this was not a useful line of discussion, but I couldn't help myself. I kept thinking of the what if's and was annoyed and terrified.

"I couldn't sleep and wanted to work the puzzle. I was so cold sitting in the road. I tried to stand up, but I couldn't. I sat there, hoping you would help me up and back into the house. It was so cold; I was really scared."

"I can imagine-well, no. I really can't imagine. I need to take you to the ER. The cuts are too deep for me to deal with. Do you want anything to eat or drink before we go?"

"No. I'm okay. Just let me get a bit warm first."

We drove twenty minutes to the hospital as the sun was beginning to make its presence known.

"That was pretty stupid what I did," Deloris acknowledged.

"Yep."

Conflicting emotions swirled around in my head. Concern about whether Deloris had suffered any lasting damage fought for space with wondering if I could have done anything to prevent the accident. My main reaction was one of disbelief; I couldn't comprehend what had made Deloris decide to go outside in the middle of the night without a flashlight. She'd said she was scared sitting in the middle of a cold, dark road, unable to stand up. She must have been scared. I know I would have been.

"I should have taken a flashlight. Then I could have seen the way better. Of course, if I had my car keys, I would have driven, very slowly, to my 7:00 a.m. meeting."

"What meeting?" I asked, knowing there wasn't one.

"I can't remember," Deloris said. A few minutes later, she added, "Driving would have been pretty foolish, wouldn't it?"

"Yep. Sure would've." It was hard to consider Deloris driving.

An exam and a CAT scan in the ER indicated she had a broken nose as well as lacerations on her forehead, eye, and the inside of her lower lip. No other damage, physical or neurological, was noted.

The doctor told Deloris, "Your forehead looks shredded. I'm going to give you some local anesthesia to deaden the pain and then clean out the cuts and stitch you up." He told her the injections might hurt a little because they would be made directly into the cuts, and that turned out to be an understatement.

Deloris howled as the needle was inserted into her forehead. Writhing on the exam table, she repeatedly pleaded, "STOP! THAT HURTS! OW! STOP."

"Easy, hon. Take deep breaths. I'm here. Hold onto my hand and squeeze it when you hurt." I attempted to calm her as the nurse and I held her steady and the doctor completed the injections. As the anesthesia took effect, Deloris calmed down and relaxed enough to allow herself to be cleaned and sutured. Her face black and blue, she was given prescriptions for some oral antibiotics. We returned home. She went to bed. A cup of coffee in hand, I sat pondering the morning's events and wondering how to keep something like that from happening ever again.

After examining her the next day, Dr. Gehrke confirmed that Deloris had not suffered any new seizures, strokes, or other neurological damage. Aside from some contusions and lacerations, her only injury was a broken nose. The trauma probably slowed the progress of her neurological recovery.

Hallucinations followed the incident as well as a noticeable increase in confabulations. Deloris was sure other people were living in the house. In fact, she was convinced we were actually living in someone else's house, although it looked very much like ours. "I can't believe you were able to move all our stuff to this house and set it up like it was at home," she said. "I'm really impressed. But whose house is it? How did you get them to let us live here?"

"It's our house, hon. We live here."

Deloris refused to believe my assurances. Since it didn't seem to bother her to be living in what she thought was a "cloned house," I let it go.

Along with increased mobility, as she recovered from her fall, Deloris experienced a shift in her sleeping habits. One night I was sitting at my computer about 1:30 a.m., doing some writing, when Deloris came down the stairs. She seemed confused. "Why is it so dark?" she asked. "It's 1:30 in the afternoon."

"Actually, hon, it's 1:30 in the morning. That's why it's dark. You should probably be in bed. So should I, truth be told."

"I'm hungry. And I want to watch some TV."

I got her some cookies and a cup of tea, helped her get situated in front of the TV, locked up the house, and went to bed. Several hours later, glaring lights in the bedroom woke me up; Deloris had apparently turned on the overhead lights in the bedroom and was saying something about Queen Nefertiti's mummy that, in my more-asleep-than-awake state, I did not understand. She got back into bed then and promptly fell asleep, leaving me wide awake and wondering how to get our sleep patterns back in sync, and what Queen Nefertiti had to do with anything.

When her nose was set and her face began to heal, she no longer looked like the victim of vicious domestic abuse. Rather, her face looked like a cross between a Japanese Kabuki mask and a raccoon. Having the stitches removed improved her spirits. Her pain was manageable with Tylenol, which allowed her to return to writing and a desire to do more around the house. Although I had to keep her focused in both activities, as she tended to become distracted, I was relieved that she was once again progressing.

"I'm Sorry. I Can't Do It."

"Hello, Allan. This is Johsel Namkung," said the voice on the other end of the telephone line. A world famous Korean-American photographer, Johsel was an old friend of Deloris's. His candid photo of Deloris taken at our wedding sits framed on my desk. "There is going to be a retrospective of my work at the Museum of Northwest Art, and I would like Deloris to write the catalog."

"I know she'd love to work with you, Johsel, and be honored you asked. However, I don't know if you've heard-Deloris had a stroke about four months ago. And, to be honest with you, I'm not sure she's able to focus well enough to do the work. She won't tell you this, though."

"I didn't know. I'm so sorry. I will consider this when I talk with her."

As I expected, Deloris told Johsel she would be happy to write the piece. I knew she felt she could do it. I, on the other hand, had serious doubts. When the two of them met and went over slides and ideas, Deloris was her old professional self, at least during the first part of the conversation. She asked good questions and suggested creative approaches. After about thirty minutes, she lost focus. Luckily, Johsel had known what to expect and was not concerned.

In the weeks that followed, Deloris was blasé about her ability to meet the catalog's deadline. My reminders that she had made a commitment to a friend who was counting on her did not create any sense of urgency. In retrospect, I think they may have had the opposite effect.

As the deadline neared, I became increasingly concerned about her ability to follow through. I repeatedly urged her to call Johsel. "You need to tell him you can't complete the piece. He needs time to find someone else to do it."

"I have never missed a deadline," she said.

"I know, hon. But that was before. You are a different person now. And Johsel is your friend; this is important to him."

For whatever reasons, I had become so invested in Deloris's behavior that I felt her failure would reflect not only on her but on me as well. The more stubborn she became about her ability to finish the project, the angrier I became at her refusal to recognize and accept what I perceived as her new reality.

"Have you done any work on Johsel's book?" I asked several days later, as Deloris reclined on the day bed, magazine in hand.

"I will."

"You've been saying that for months and all you have written is one paragraph. The deadline is only a week or two away. He's your friend. You can't let him down."

"I won't."

"So when are you going to do some work?"

"Don't worry about it. I'll get it done."

"I really doubt it. Call him, damn it, like I have asked you to. If you don't, I will."

"Don't. I can do this."

"No, actually, you can't. It's not your fault. Your brain is not functioning the way it has in the past. You can't pull this together. I really wish you could. Just pick up the damned phone and call Johsel. He'll understand. You have to give him enough time to get someone else to work on it."

My pleas received a stone-faced, silent reply and increased intransigence, which made me even angrier. The downward spiral continued. It was a scenario that would play out a number of times in different contexts during the ensuing months and years, as we both struggled to adapt to Deloris's altered abilities.

Then Susan, Deloris's speech therapist, suggested she give up the project, and Deloris readily agreed this would be the wise course of action. She even had someone in mind to complete it, which made it easier for her to make the call to Johsel. As it happened, he had already realized what was happening and had decided that, with a few slight additions, he could use what Deloris had written about him in her earlier book, Iridescent Light. In that way, Deloris could be part of the catalog, which he wanted, without having to write anything new, which she wasn't in this moment in a position to do.

As on many occasions before and since, I was touched by people's concern and caring for Deloris. I also learned, once again, that messages from someone other than me were easier for Deloris to hear and accept. When someone else made a suggestion, the emotional load she and I carried for each other didn't come into play.

Susan described Deloris as being in the transition stage between pre-stroke and post-stroke. This concept was strange to me as I considered all the time after the incident as being post-stroke. Susan explained there was a period of indeterminate duration after the actual event during which changes and recovery take place as the person develops new patterns of behavior and new ways of interfacing with the world around them. At some point, the person settles into a post-stroke persona, which becomes relatively stable. A second, or even third, transition stage could occur later. Deloris was still in the initial transition stage.

I found this concept personally useful. It was an optimistic model, containing the implicit potential of continued transformation and change. I didn't know how long this transition period could last or when it might end. I presumed it to be different for each individual. My previous research indicated most recovery took place in the first six months. As Deloris reached that pivotal time, Susan's comments about transitions were comforting. Deloris's recovery was proceeding along normal patterns, and more progress was possible.

Overall, I thought Deloris was dealing with this new reality better than I would have in her situation. In fact, she was probably doing better than I was at the time. I was very concerned about my anger, as it was not an emotion I had experienced, or at least expressed, much before Deloris's stroke. Now, I was often angry, especially when I felt challenged or experienced a loss of control. Part of me didn't want to be in control and resented feeling the need to be so. Yet, Deloris needed help, guidance, and protection, which in my mind, translated into my needing to exert control.

It was a major shift from the equality and mutual decision-making we had previously experienced in our marriage. Neither of us was totally comfortable with this shift in our power relationship. I began to realize I was going to need some professional help with this; I needed therapy.

November 6, 2005

We had some firsts today-a late brunch at the Smiling Dog, after a trip to Bayview Arts, and some time on her computer. Deloris has been talking about wanting to research some things but can never remember what they are. This afternoon she went into her desk, sat down, and turned on the computer. She wanted to look up some idea about Dracula that she had-still into vampires! Not sure how successful the research was because when I checked with her a short time later, she had become distracted by the opportunity to watch some previews of new movies on a different website. She seemed to be enjoying herself and was at least able to handle the computer at a level of proficiency that worked for her. Brunch was easy.

I installed another grab bar. I attempted to install a handheld shower for Deloris, but the equipment was faulty. I couldn't get it to stop leaking. I have to return it and get another one. The other grab bar I bought is too long for the available space, so that, too, has to be exchanged. And then, I guess I will have to bite the bullet and actually drill through the ceramic shower tile to install grab bars in our upstairs shower. I know it is probably easier than I perceive it to be; however, I have these visions of destroying the tile and not being able to replace the squares. I have not been able to find anyone who can help me in this project; hard to say whether they would be able to do it any better than I, but at least if they mess up, I have someone else to blame. Always makes me feel better.

Finding the right balance between giving Deloris independence and maintaining a tight leash is difficult. At times it strains us both. She chafes at being told what to do all the time-at least that is her perspective. I'm scared that she will hurt herself as a result of my letting down my vigilance or allowing her too much freedom. She is much more capable than she was even ten days ago but much less than she thinks. I'm becoming frustrated when she does not act with the speed I want. Deloris, on the other hand, thinks that I am being a dictator- and may well be digging in her heels, metaphorically speaking, to claim some personal autonomy. This evening I jokingly told her that she was acting as stubborn as her Aunt Kay. She understood that if my comment was serious, either it was a major insult or she was being mulish in her behavior. I am confident that, as this situation continues, we will continue to make adjustments so that these conflicts lessen in number and intensity.

Deloris continues to be my teacher. While I sometimes fight this, I am learning patience, being of service to others, and acceptance. These are just some of the lessons I am learning from being with my wife. We have only just begun, and I am exhausted. I don't know how people do this for months and years. Hopefully, I won't have to find out; just as hopefully, if I do have to find out, I will find out how to do it. And do it with grace, as well as grit.I don't remember whether physical therapy starts tomorrow or Tuesday. I guess I will find out tomorrow.

Allan

CHAPTER SEVEN
ONE PADDLE, TWO PADDLE: STRATEGIES FOR COPING

Piaget Revisited

PERSEVERANCE FURTHERS, the I Ching, an ancient Taoist text, advises. A journey of a thousand miles begins with one step; then another; and yet another, according to an old saying. Don Ho sings, "One paddle, two paddle, three paddle, four" as he describes a canoeist returning to his home. Whichever metaphor you choose, it describes my focus to keep on keepin' on in my caring for Deloris. To do that, it was clear I needed help dealing with my anger.

John Bayley describes a discovery he made about his own anger in Elegy for Iris, a memoir about caring for his wife, the author Iris Murdoch, as she descended into Alzheimer's. Bayley found that his anger might be a way of refusing to admit anything was wrong. He had a point. A rational person doesn't get angry with someone for failing to do what she is incapable of doing. Was I refusing to see that Deloris was incapable of the level of independence I wanted for her?

Even when I felt Deloris was doing something intentionally to anger me, at some level I knew that wasn't what was happening. That's a funny concept-deciding rationally that a feeling you're experiencing is irrational. I did believe her behavior at times was conscious and intentional, "you can't make me do this, and I won't." Mostly, however, she was at the mercy of her neurological functions. Intellectually I knew this; emotionally, I needed things to be different. So I acted as if my desires could be actualized by sheer force of will. At some primal level, I felt that if I allowed her inabilities to motivate my response, Deloris would never get better; she would never achieve the level of independence I desired for her. I knew this was irrational and could lead to self-defeating behavior and mindsets. Yet I could not seem to accept what I saw before me.

I was exhausted to my core. I was often on the verge of tears. Just under my anger was an ocean of grief. While I could usually control the weeping, sometimes it broke through. Alone, late at night, the crying seemed to be cathartic. After the tears had flowed, however, I could see that crying had increased my frustration and made me more conscious of loss. When I was willing to admit it, I knew I was depressed. My doctor offered to prescribe antidepressants. I had taken some years before and hadn't liked the way they made me feel. Rather than eliminating depression, the medication had blocked my ability to sense it. My depression was still there; it just existed on the other side of a semi-permeable filter.

When I mentioned this sensation, the doctor assured me that he had in mind a different class of medication. I knew I needed something, and acknowledged the drugs might be helpful. If the results were different from my earlier experience, I would feel no worse for having taken them. So, I began taking Prozac. It seemed to help, but my anxiety and extreme sense of loss persisted. I needed other strategies to cope.

I had worked with therapists in the past when I felt overwhelmed and unable to cope with events in my life. The aftermath of Deloris's stroke had turned my life upside down. I could no longer do what I wanted, when I wanted, limited by the respect and mutuality Deloris and I had for each other. Now, I was committed to caring for Deloris, a 24/7 responsibility. I needed new skills for this new job. Those I had honed as a lawyer and higher education administrator were not applicable. Marx Brothers movies, self-medicating with wine and martinis, and vegetating in front of a TV set were means of escape. They were not helpful or effective as long-term strategies. In actuality they were manifestations of the problems I was facing.

In April 2006, eight months after Deloris's stroke, I entered therapy with Leah Green. I felt comfortable with both her professional capabilities and personal compassion. Through our work together, I realized I was mourning the loss of the woman I had married and with whom I had shared a life. Leah, who worked with Iraqi war veterans suffering from severe forms of post-traumatic stress disorder (PTSD,) considered my grief a manifestation of that condition. She helped me realize I had suffered a major shock, with resultant trauma.

Treatments appropriate for PTSD might be useful to me as well. Her office was a safe space for me to let down my shields, express my fears and vulnerabilities, cry, and grieve my loss.

Leah recommended a book, Growing Up Again: Parenting Ourselves, Parenting Our Children, written by Jean Ilsey Clarke and Connie Dawson. The authors, two therapists, posit that adults recovering from brain injuries go through similar cognitive developmental stages the psychologist Jean Piaget describes in children. So, when I told Leah, "Sometimes the way Deloris acts, I think I am married to a two-year-old," there was validity in my observation. Deloris was re-experiencing the cognitive development of a two-year-old as she struggled to regain lost capacities. While that knowledge did not entirely ease my frustration or dissipate my anger when Deloris refused to perform the simple tasks I asked of her, I better understood what was happening. She was exerting her independence and individuality in the only way she knew-by reliving her "terrible twos." Given this new understanding, and the knowledge Deloris was on the road to recovery, helped me appreciate what both of us were going through.

For myself, I saw that I was living with the delusion that I could heal my wife with the very strength of my intention. I am the first grandchild of immigrant grandparents, and a boy child at that. My grandparents thought it quite natural, therefore, to consider me as an incarnation of the Messiah. I certainly recommend anyone wishing to develop high self-esteem to receive this type of early childhood adoration. As much as I wanted to believe my grandparents' perceptions were accurate (my parents certainly knew better), it is clear they were not. I might want to be able to heal Deloris by the force of my will and desire, but I could not do so.

The unwavering belief I held that Deloris could, and would, get better was a source of strength and optimism, but it also led to disappointment and frustration for us both. Leah helped me realize the incredible burden I had placed on myself, and on Deloris, by holding onto this belief. Once I realized I couldn't make Deloris better by wishing it so, or attempting to control her behavior, the relief for both of us was palpable. I was able to recognize that Deloris wanted to get better and would do so, but only on her own time and in her own manner. My job was to support her in any and every way I could, to be a loving coach and cheerleader, and to act as her memory and calendar when such was required. I did not have control over the timing or process of her improvement. As hard as accepting this reality was for this control-freak former trial attorney, my doing so was vital and liberating for both of us.

A friend gave me a copy of Ken Wilber's book, Grace and Grit, in which he and his wife, Treya, write of the struggles and joys involved in her experience with cancer. She had received her diagnosis just weeks after their marriage, and until she succumbed to cancer five years later, the two of them lived the experience together. The philosopher Ken Wilber is a deep thinker and prolific writer, and I had read-or attempted to read-his other books, which I found to be challenging and dense. Grace and Grit, on the other hand, was personal, written from the heart. His reaction to the initial diagnosis was as stark as my own.

> *Strange things happen to the mind when catastrophe strikes. It felt like the universe turned into a thin paper tissue, and then someone simply tore the tissue in half right in front of my eyes. I was so stunned that it was as if absolutely nothing had happened. A tremendous strength descended on me, the strength of being both totally jolted and totally stupefied. I was clear, present, and very determined. (p. 34)*

I could see in his writing how the five years Wilber lived on this journey toward his wife's death had matured him. I sensed I could learn from him. And I sensed that if Wilber's travail had changed him, mine might change me as well.

Allan Time

At the same time I was dealing with anger and grief, I also experienced bouts of fear. I constantly worried something would happen to Deloris: she would hurt herself in a fall, have another stroke, or something I had not identified would cause her to be even more incapacitated than she presently was. My major fear, however, was that something would happen to me. Who would take care of Deloris then?

Everything I read on caregiving contained the same advice: take care of yourself first so you can take care of your loved one. I knew the advice was spot on. I watched what I ate, went to the gym when I could, and slept when I was able. Yet when I looked in the mirror, what I saw reflected back was an aging, exhausted face. Friends gave me the same message. "You need to take better care of yourself. What are you doing for fun?"

The question dumbfounded me. If I was really concerned about something happening to me, why wasn't I taking better care of myself? Why wasn't I looking for ways to at least let off a little steam?

The husband of a teaching colleague suffered from Alzheimer's disease. When his condition got to be more than she could handle, she told me she sat at the bottom of their backyard swimming pool and screamed at the top of her lungs until she was exhausted. We didn't have a pool, or even a backyard hot tub. So, while I liked the visual image her story evoked, I needed a different strategy. I knew screaming at Deloris-something that seemed to be happening more and more often-was both inappropriate and unloving. Even worse, it was not an effective stress reducer. Just the opposite, actually.

"I'm worried about you," Deloris said one day. "You need to get away and do something." I was surprised at her ability to recognize what was happening and appreciated her sensitivity to my situation. I needed to regain some semblance of my pre-stroke life.

Time apart from Deloris, leaving her alone, had begun with baby steps-a half hour away to run errands, a short walk in the neighborhood. I was happy to be out and about on my own, yet concerned about what I would find when I returned home. Each time I walked through the door, I was relieved to find Deloris comfortable, sometimes even unaware I had been gone. I bought walkie-talkies so I could be on the deck or in the yard and Deloris could contact me. We never figured out how they worked, so while a good idea, it was a failed experiment.

Something else was required.

During the first months following Deloris's return home from the hospital, I had been unwilling to have any outsider care for her. It made no difference if they were friend, family, or professional. It was not from any desire I had to be a martyr nor a belief I could do it better than anyone else. Rather, I feared I would never forgive myself if something happened to Deloris while someone else was in charge. Even though I had no training or experience as a caregiver (in fact, did not really know what I was doing), I believed the responsibility for

Deloris's care was mine and mine alone. In time, I had to admit I couldn't keep rowing this canoe without help.

Employing outside caregivers for Deloris was essential for us both. I sought recommendations from friends and referrals from the South Whidbey Senior Center. I involved Deloris in all the interviews, as she was the one who would be spending time with and being dependent upon a caregiver. After the basics of experience, availability, and references, neither of us knew what to ask or what we wanted to know from these applicants. Interpersonal chemistry seemed important. Deloris had to feel comfortable with that person. Deloris had to feel like she could have an enjoyable and intelligent discussion with her caregiver, who would respect not only our property but also our lifestyle and ideas. Some of the people were friends of friends, a condition which made the process a bit easier, personalizing the options. With few exceptions, Deloris liked her caregivers. All were reliable and responsible. Sometimes, they became her friends.

Having the support of a caregiver gave me more physical and emotional freedom. I took walks on the beach, saw friends, played golf-as I describe it, "planting golf ball trees,"-or took naps. The caregivers cooked a bit, washed clothes, and did light housecleaning. They entertained Deloris by sharing movies on TV and conversations. It was well worth the expense to relieve some of the stress Deloris and I were both experiencing.

Still, my life was off balance. This became clear when I realized most of my social life was seeing people at the meetings of nonprofits in which I was involved. The great majority of the people I served with were friends, and I did appreciate being able to put my energy into something other than caregiving and teaching-but I needed more. I needed a different diversion, something that was pure enjoyment, and I needed a longer break.

One day one of my sisters-in-law called to tell me that she and the other sister-in-law were planning a girls' week with Deloris, and I had to leave. Ruth and Karen were traveling halfway across the country on this outing. "We're coming to see Deloris, and you need to leave," was the way Ruth put it-unspoken, but present, were the words "and have a much-needed vacation."

Where I went and what I did during this break assumed an importance of its own. I knew I wanted sunshine, warmth, maybe a beach, and definitely pampering. I decided against Club Med or a cruise, which, while satisfying some of the requirements I had established for the break, were best enjoyed in the company of another person. I didn't want a travel companion. Ultimately, the perfect solution occurred to me: I called our friends Roger and Gayle in Hawaii and invited myself there for a visit.

I first met Roger in 1970, several months after I moved to Seattle. It didn't take long for us to become loyal and lifelong friends. Over the years, we worked together, dated some of the same women-although seldom at the same time-shared good times and bad. He lived in a cabin on my Bainbridge Island property before moving to Hawaii. In the three-plus decades he has been in the Pacific, we have visited back and forth numerous times. He attended both my weddings, as well as my sixtieth birthday party in 2002, where he was a big hit dressed in a French maid's costume, which complemented his bearded face and short, rotund body. I officiated at his and Gayle's wedding. Even with the distance separating us, the four of us have been close, intimate friends. And while I was concerned Deloris might be resentful of my visiting Roger and Gayle without her, I was confident Karen and Ruth's visit would be an ideal substitute. Which it was.

Roger, Gayle, and I camped in an Oahu-beachfront park. All I did was sleep, eat, drink, play games, swim, and walk the beach. I wasn't allowed to cook, clean, or assume any responsibility other than relaxing and enjoying myself. It was wonderful. I felt pampered, loved, and cared for by my friends. At the end of the much-too-short week, I was re-energized, refreshed, and almost ready to return to my obligations on the mainland. Equally energizing was the knowledge, from my phone calls home, that Deloris was also having a wonderful time.

"Hi, hon. What's happening?" I asked her on one of my evening calls.

"Hello, love. We're just about to eat. Karen and Ruth cooked this amazing dinner. And then we're going to drink some wine and watch a DVD."

"What are you going to watch?"

"I don't remember. I gotta go. Love you."

"You too." I said, but she'd already disconnected. I smiled as I hung up the phone. Deloris had always liked talking to me on the phone, even when we didn't have anything special to say to each other, and her rush to get off that day was a sign to me that she was enjoying herself and was missing me less than she did when I previously was away from home. She was with her family, women she knew and loved, and she was having a great time.

"She's good," I reported to Roger and Gayle and reached out to accept the martini he'd just mixed for me.

When I returned home, I put more energy into another outlet I'd been developing over the months of Deloris's recovery time at home: writing. Writing filled a creative need for me, and it also served a number of other purposes. Immediately after Deloris's stroke, I started emailing daily updates to family and friends. Most evenings, I sat at my computer and reflected on the events of the day-how Deloris was doing, how I was feeling, what news the doctors had given us. Over the months the email lists grew, as friends asked to be included and began forwarding them to their friends. At the same time, the content morphed from informative to reflective, as the emails became my journal entries.

Writing gave me a way to sort through everything that was happening and attempt to make sense out of it. It also gave me a way of staying in communication, albeit one-sided, with people I cared about-though it didn't matter if these people responded to my emails or even read them. I wrote for my own purposes. That other people read these emails, that I was living my emotional life in public, was a secondary consideration. Ultimately, the benefits to me of writing the emails and the encouragement I received from the friends and family who did read them gave rise to this book.

I enrolled in some writing classes and joined a critique group. I had been writing all my life, although almost never what is termed "creative writing." In my law practice, I wrote letters, briefs, contracts, and opinion drafts for the decision-makers for whom I worked. Some of this was certainly creative, though it never sounded creative. I do say I gave up writing fiction when I stopped practicing law. As a teacher, I wrote course syllabi, class lesson plans, and comments on my students' papers. I had published a couple of short pieces in a professional journal and written some vignettes based on experiences in my earlier years. Also, I had kept a journal for years, sometimes regularly but most often writing in it only in times of struggle and trauma-which is precisely what this situation was.

For me writing was neither discipline nor vocation. My wife was the professional writer; I just wrote. Now the circumstances were reversed. Deloris could barely comprehend other people's writing, and what she wrote herself were fragments, disconnected and often incomprehensible. I was becoming the writer, thanks in part to the suggestions I received from my teachers and members of my writers' group. These were invaluable in helping me to develop writing skills and allowing me to feel more like a well-rounded human being.

Nonmonetary Benefits

Shortly after Deloris and I moved to Whidbey Island, I resigned my full-time position as a higher education administrator with the University of Phoenix and began teaching online courses for the school. This shift in professional focus allowed me to work from home, at my convenience, and enjoy living on Whidbey. The tasks involved teaching and class preparation, communicating with students, and grading papers. While not necessarily what I wanted to do for fun, these responsibilities provided a release from the pressures of caregiving. Schoolwork could be, and often was, done late at night or at other times when Deloris was asleep. In addition to the intellectual stimulation, I was able to earn needed money through teaching. I was also able to help Deloris take care of her aunt and then, after her stroke, to care for Deloris.

My teaching responsibilities with the University of Phoenix involved periodic weeklong trips out of town, mainly to Phoenix, and, on occasion, to Atlanta or Washington, D.C. These assignments paid more than online classes and gave me a chance to visit family and friends. They also required making logistical arrangements-finding someone to stay with Deloris while I was away. Sometimes family members were able to help shoulder the load. Deloris enjoyed this enormously as it gave her one-on-one time with her sister, her daughter, and her sisters-in-law, and helped to strengthen the bonds between her and the women in her life. Such experiences, I believed, contributed in real, though indefinable, ways to Deloris's continued healing. My mind was at rest as well, because I was confident my wife was being well cared for and having fun when women whom she loved and who loved her were visiting.

When family members were not available, several of Deloris's local caregivers were willing to stay overnight while I was away. Even though these arrangements substantially cut into the money I earned from the trip, the nonmonetary benefits to both Deloris and me were substantial. Getting a break from each other helped us realize how dependent on me Deloris had become-and also how much we valued each other's company. My trips gave me opportunities to share time with friends, engage in intellectual discussions not presently possible with Deloris, and receive compliments and recognition not only for the work I was doing with Deloris but for my professional endeavors.

When I was out of town, I called home daily--both to check in with the caregiver and to talk with Deloris. Most of these conversations with Deloris were similar in nature. She called me one day in the middle of class. I called her back during our next break.

"Hi, hon. I was in the middle of class when you called. What's up?"

"When are you going to be home?" she asked.

"I'm in Phoenix." This was about the fifth time I'd reminded her of this in the two days since I had left. "I'll be home Tuesday-four days from now."

"I thought you were going to pick me up," Deloris said.

"Where was I going to take you?"

"Home."

"You are home."

"No, I'm not. I'm on Whidbey, and we live in Seattle." This had been a recurrent theme since her stroke. At times she was perfectly cognizant of where we lived; at other times, she was certain we still lived in the home we had in Seattle.

"Not anymore," I said. "We're Islanders now. We moved to Whidbey about five years ago. It was your idea. We sold our house on Fullerton to Kevin, our neighbor. Don't you remember?"

There was a long pause before Deloris said, "Oh, right. I remember." Another long pause. "So, when are you going to be home?"

"Late Tuesday night, long after you go to bed. Today's Friday, so that's four days from now. I'll wake you when I get home."

"I look forward to it."

"So do I. Caregivers working out?"

"They're fine. Everything's good. I just miss you."

"You too. Love you. Bye for now."

"Bye."

Was my wife re-experiencing the inability to project into the future that's common among young children gaining levels of cognitive development? I often sensed an underlying sadness in our out-of-town phone conversations. Deloris had grown extremely dependent, emotionally and physically, on my presence in her life. Caregivers could, and did, satisfy many of the physical needs; her emotional needs were more difficult. We both recognized my out-of-town trips as being mutually valuable; but they carried downsides and costs, emotional and psychic as well as monetary. Yet on balance, I considered the benefits to be well worth the costs.

However I was able to do it, carving out time to work, to engage in intellectually stimulating activities, and to interact socially with other people are crucial caregiving survival strategies. The long-term, one-paddle-two-paddle steadiness that kept my canoe going forward was difficult without the buoyancy personal time provided.

You Got to Have Friends

Ultimately, I found the strongest and most important strategy for learning to float was, and is, to have friends and to maintain social interactions. Isolation breeds loneliness and ultimately depression. Becoming mired in my own story to the exclusion of everyone else's can result in an inability to function, in resenting what I perceive to be the cause of this situation-in my case, Deloris's reduced capacities. Even though my contact was primarily through email and phone calls, I valued maintaining friendships and sought out opportunities for interaction with others.

About a year after returning home, Deloris started going to the local Senior Center three days a week. There she could develop new friendships and have her own social interactions. I scheduled lunches and walks with friends during these breaks in my caregiving responsibilities. These connections made me feel some normalcy was returning to my life. The inherent insular nature of life on South Whidbey-it was a small community on an island after all-encouraged the development of relationships with what Seattle-based therapist Marv Thomas calls "familiar strangers." These people, who appear in our lives on a somewhat regular basis either because of their relationships with others (think degrees of separation) or the roles they play in our lives (e.g., the cashier at the grocery store, the librarian, physical therapists, doctors) add another important layer of social dimension. It wasn't that I had deep or personal connections with any of these people; I didn't. Yet I would see them with some regularity, or perhaps interact with them with a cordiality that provided a type of comfort I enjoyed, and perhaps needed.

I moved from the East Coast to the Northwest because I did not want to live through any more cold, icy winters. Then in December of 2006, I returned from a business trip to Atlanta, where the weather was so cold a walk across the hotel parking lot was more than I could handle; what awaited me at home on Whidbey was even worse. The streets were slick with ice, frost covered the trees, and, most disturbing, the electricity was out. A major wind and ice storm had moved through the area, taking down power lines and plunging all of Whidbey Island, along with much of Seattle and surrounding areas, into unheated darkness. For almost five days, we had no heat, lights, or-since the pump is electric-running water. Deloris spent much of the time huddled under blankets, wearing a coat, hat, and gloves. I was only slightly more mobile. Since we had a gas stove, I was able to cook and make coffee. Some friends near Seattle had regained power several days later, and when I called, invited us to come and stay with them. When we arrived, they greeted us with hugs, warmth, and great food and wine.

The next morning, refreshed and warmed by both heat and friendship, we returned home, hoping to find power restored. No such luck. Our house remained dark and very cold. A motel in Coupeville, twenty miles away, had power and vacancies, so I reserved a room. I wanted Deloris to be warm and more comfortable than she had been in our lightless, heatless home.

A few hours later, as I attempted to coax some heat from our propane-powered fireplace, the phone rang.

"Hi, Allan. This is Bev Rose." We had met Bev at a potluck about a month earlier. She lived several miles away on the other side of the highway that runs the length of the Island. "We've got heat, lights, food on the stove, and a house full of fascinating people. Come on over."

I immediately accepted, thankful for the generous invitation. Cold and tired, we arrived at Bev's house, which was filled with light, laughter, the aroma of food, and, thankfully, heat. It was Hanukkah, the Jewish Festival of Light-an irony since most of Whidbey Island remained in the dark. Candles were burning at Bev's house; potato latkes, a traditional food for the Hanukkah holiday, were being fried.

We were made to feel welcome, greeted as members of a caring community, many of whom were strangers to us before that evening.

Later that evening our hostess gave us yet another generous invitation. Learning we were planning to drive to Coupeville to spend the night in a motel, Bev asked her daughter and granddaughter to share a bed so Deloris and I could sleep in the granddaughter's bed. Our protests about not wanting to inconvenience them were ignored, and we spent the night, grateful for the kindness. The lessons of that Hanukkah taught that even on the darkest night (and in the most inconvenient of circumstances), there is light; it comes in the form of support from friends, old and new.

The following year, in late summer I was attempting to resolve a perceived dilemma. I was scheduled to teach a weeklong class in Seattle at the same time a reunion was planned for a group of friends from our high school's B'nai B'rith Youth Organization. I had known some of these men literally all my life. One of them was born in the same hospital, two days before me. Our mothers' rooms were down the hall from each other. Our brothers were friends; their sons were friends; our fathers had been friendly competitors in the same profession. This classmate was married to a woman I had dated in high school. Others in the group I had known since grade school. We had gone through puberty together, dated many of the same women, and suffered together through the agonies of adolescence. After college, we scattered across the country, and now we spanned it-from Vermont to Southern California, from Washington State to South Florida. In the past forty years, we had only been together as a group twice, the first time in 1997 and the second a few years after.

I wanted to go to that reunion and I also wanted to teach the course. I couldn't be in two places at the same time, and I felt torn. One day at breakfast I outlined the situation to Deloris and asked her thoughts.

"Do whatever you want," she said off-handedly, her attention apparently riveted on a newspaper headline.

My initial response was frustration, but I had to admit that wasn't fair. Deloris was cognitively incapable of shutting out other input sufficiently to focus on my question. She was easily distracted by whatever crossed her field of vision and, as she'd always said, she was "attracted to the written word." So, I reminded myself that my wife was not purposely avoiding being of assistance. Before her stroke, we had always discussed matters of importance to either of us and made joint decisions, or at least solicited input from each other. As I thought about it, I was glad I'd asked. It was almost enough that Deloris had recovered sufficiently for me to consider talking this over with her. Though initially unsatisfying, it felt like a baby step back to that kind of exchange.

Considering her response further-do whatever you want-I realized Deloris had resolved my dilemma. Which of the two options did I want most? The answer to that was whichever of them would make me feel more whole, more of an individual. When I phrased the issue in those terms, I knew the answer.

The next day at breakfast I asked, "Hon, do you remember me wondering whether to go to Louisville or teach the residency in Seattle?"

"Sure."

"I decided I am going to Louisville. It'll be fun to see my old buddies and share stories and lies about high school. And I could see my brother Mark and maybe his kids. The class in Seattle is convenient and the money would be nice. I would enjoy the teaching, but the trip to Louisville will really be fun. "

"Good," she said. "You should go."

And so, after making arrangements for someone to stay with my wife, that's what I did.

The first morning we were in Louisville, we sat in a circle, coffee and bagels in hand. One of the weekend's organizers welcomed us and said we would start the weekend with a sharing circle.

I was sitting about a quarter of the way around the circle from the first speaker. The guys before me were very upbeat; they spoke one by one about vacations and work. When it was my turn, I took a deep breath and paused for a moment before starting to speak. Should I talk about Deloris's condition and my caregiving role right now? In this group? If I did, what I had to say would change the energy in the room. It would dampen the jocularity and lightness with which we had started the weekend. But these were some of my oldest and dearest friends. Certainly sharing what was happening in my life, the hardships as well as the joys, was the right step to take.

"Most of you have never met my wife, Deloris," I began. "We met over twenty years ago at a friend's party, watching the Kentucky Derby and drinking mint juleps." I added that for local color. "In August 2005 she suffered a stroke, and I have been her primary caregiver ever since. It's been a difficult and frustrating two years, but

I'm happy to say she's sufficiently recovered that I am comfortable leaving her with a professional caregiver and being here with y'all this weekend."

I spoke a little further about the challenges, and my eyes filled with tears as I talked. I felt fortunate that I was able to complete my sharing without either crying or having my voice crack. I felt a tremendous emotional release sharing with these people, men with whom I had a bond so strong it would not-I think, could not-be broken. As others continued to share around the circle, it was obvious that the energy had indeed shifted; it had deepened. People spoke not only about vacation trips they'd been on but also about the illnesses of their loved ones, legal troubles with their ex-spouses, estrangements from their children, and concerns for their own futures. With each person's contribution to the sharing, the subtle strands that bound us together became stronger. We were re-experiencing at a deeper, more mature level the connections we had established decades earlier.

I felt as if I were being held, were being comforted in the warmth and love of these men with whom many years before I had shared and learned so much. I felt incredibly lucky, blessed even, to have such male friends in my life-men with whom I felt comfortable enough to be vulnerable and who would, in return, share with me at a deep emotional level. It is not what men are said to do when they get together.

As our weekend progressed, we had our share of food and drink, laughter, jibes, stories, tall tales, and even friendly lies. I treasured those times as much as the sharing. It was all part of a whole. While we were men raised in the '50s and '60s, with shared social mores, we were more than those cultural stereotypes. We were willing to let others into our hearts, our souls, to be something other than, more than, the persona we presented to the world. We were, as we referred to each other, brothers in everything but blood.

* * *

The following year, back home on South Whidbey Island, I found another circle where the sharing was deep and personal, while interspersed with laughter and light-hearted caring. Several friends were members of a group they had formed and named the Circle of Caring. This is a close-knit group of about a dozen people who meet twice a month in each other's homes. The Circle's purpose is for its members to give support and comfort to each other through whatever joys and sorrows arise in our lives, while at the same time we explore together what it means to grow older. At the Circle's inception, about four years before I became a member, its founders observed that their children and siblings lived all over the world and, with the necessities of age coming upon them, it was helpful to organize a group of friends they could count on in times of emergency.

The group's norms and practices are these: we sit in a circle, or as close to one as the living room in which we are meeting allows. A candle is lit and a small gong rung, signifying the beginning of a short period of silent meditation. These rituals indicate we are entering a space and time separate from, and different than, that which exists outside our circle. Confidentiality is a cardinal precept-what is said inside the Circle stays inside the Circle. I requested permission from the Circle to include this description of our activities. It was granted on the condition mine be the only name and story given. Respect and attentive listening both contribute to the success of the experience.

One by one, as deeply or superficially as we are each moved, members share what is happening in our lives, both externally and internally. Once a month, a specific subject is the focus of discussion. Topics range from what we did as teenagers and the life lessons we learned from those activities to what makes us happy, to our relationship with our parents, our siblings, and our children. At one meeting, we even wrote our own obituaries.

As I became increasingly comfortable with the group's norms and developed trust with members I had not previously known, the Circle has become a safe and sacred space for me to share emotions, feelings, and fears. I can share my feelings and thoughts, both happy and sad, ask members for help and advice, and take in the honest and heartfelt response that is offered. While tears are often shed during meetings, especially as members experience serious illnesses and deaths in their families, laughter is equally present.

Initially, I was invited to join the group on my own. It was obvious from my situation of offering full support to Deloris that I could use some support myself. Later, as Deloris regained some of her abilities, she was included in the Circle as well. We are both deeply grateful for the connections and space the Circle of Caring has provided. It is appropriately named.

Responding 'Yes, And . . .'

One afternoon, Deloris showed me an announcement in our island newspaper for an improvisational comedy class that was starting on the Island. She was interested in taking it. I recognized the teacher's name; we had heard about him in a totally different context.

A year before Deloris's stroke, we had visited Costa Rica, and during the shuttle ride to the airport on our last day, the driver asked us, "Where are you from?" We went through the predictable narrowing of focus from the U.S.A. to Washington State to Whidbey Island to the town of Freeland-where, to our astonishment, this man's business partner, a handicraft importer, lived. We didn't know the partner, but now, years later, he was showing up on our screen once again as the instructor of this improv class. It seemed a good omen.

The announcement indicated students needed to have prior theater experience and to be accepted by the teacher. Deloris called him and described her background in theater, both in college and the years since. I had always liked watching improv and thought it would be fun to learn. I told him I wanted to join the class, too, and he asked if I'd done any theater.

"Not since high school," I said. "However, I have been a trial attorney and a classroom teacher. Does that count?"

He laughed. "Absolutely. That's theater. Class starts in two weeks." I was excited and looking forward to the class. I now had another creative outlet and another outside activity to share with Deloris. While I was a bit concerned about her ability to have the energy or focus to stay in the class, I was pleased she took the initiative to find out about it and encourage me to join her. Deloris had been involved in theater while in college and also as an adult. I believed the improv class could trigger familiar memories and provide its own energy for her.

The improvisational comedy class was taught in the activities room of the local assisted living facility. At the beginning of the first evening, we stood in a circle in the middle of the room for a warm-up exercise. There were eighteen in the class, most of them strangers to me. Deloris was on the other side of the circle, supporting herself with Raisin cane, and looking less than completely comfortable. The game, "One-Word Story-Story," required the players to tell a story one word at a time. The story did not have to make complete sense; when it was our turn, we just had to add a word as quickly as possible to keep the story going. It went something like this:

"The . . ."

"Young . . ."

"Owl . . ."

"Hmm . . . looked . . ."

"At . . ."

"His . . ."

"Mother . . ."

"And . . ."

"Said . . . "

I glanced at Deloris, standing three people away from the last speaker. A strong connection had existed between us since her stroke, not unlike that between a parent and infant. I felt an energy shift, which suggested to me Deloris might be having difficulty. Her legs began to give out. As I watched, she began, in slow motion, to sink to the floor. The woman next to her caught her and supported her head. Looks of uncertainty swept through the circle. Was this something Deloris was doing intentionally, expecting the class to use it as an improv cue? I knew differently.

"Don't worry. This happens." I tried to reassure everyone and myself as I dashed across the circle and knelt beside her.

"How many fingers am I holding up?" I asked Deloris.

"Three," she responded, accurately.

"Someone call 911," I heard a voice say.

"Wait," I said, continuing my quiz of Deloris. "Where are you?"

"Class?"

"What's your name?"

"Deloris."

"Do you know who I am?"

"Of course!" she said, sounding frustrated with the questions.

"Tell me what happened."

"I got too tired to stand, and my legs just gave out."

I looked up and saw one of the nursing aides from the assisted living facility in which the class was being held hurrying toward us. "We called 911. We have to do that whenever something like this happens here," she said.

"Okay, but I don't think it is really necessary." As I was saying this, Deloris, lying on her back, began to projectile vomit. I leaned over to turn her on her side so she wouldn't choke. "Well, maybe calling 911 was a good idea."

I looked at the people around us. Their faces conveyed confusion and concern. This was not how any of us had expected to be spending our first evening together. It certainly was not the recommended way to make new friends. "No worries, people. This happens a lot. She'll be fine," I said, reassuring my classmates, and myself. My diagnosis was confirmed by the EMTs when they arrived a little while later. After they examined her and left, I took her home.

It soon became clear the physical requirements of the class were more than Deloris could comfortably handle and she stopped attending after a few more sessions. Improv became my activity. It gave me new friends with whom to play and act like a kid, opportunities to laugh and be laughed at, and permission to express myself in silly and childish ways I had not used for many years.

I also learned to accept that whatever was occurring as we worked with each other was an offer, something which advances the action or the exchange. The only appropriate response to an offer during an improve scene is, "Yes, and . . . ."I have found the same answer to work in other aspects of life as well.

In my teaching and my writing, I have often been motivated by a quotation from writing instructor William Zinsser, which has a place of honor above my desk:

I want to make people laugh so that they will see things seriously.

I wanted to-needed to-laugh to take my mind off the seriousness of my situation, to give myself some relief, while releasing the endorphins that would help me stay healthy. So, perhaps, my corollary to Zinsser's statement is I want to laugh so I won't always see things so seriously. Improv classes provided an effective alternative to the stresses of other parts of my life. I laughed, made others laugh, shared in ephemeral, unscripted, and unexpected comedic moments. Such events spontaneously appearing in one moment and disappearing the next seemed an apt metaphor for my life. What upset me in one moment might make me laugh in the next. The structure of my life, currently filled with caring for Deloris, was ever present in my mind. How I related to this structure-whether I faced it with joy or anger, whether I resented the responsibility or felt blessed by the opportunity it provided-depended upon my attitude in the moment.

Could I accept Deloris's condition and behavior and say, "Yes, and . . ."? It is a lesson I am still struggling to incorporate into my daily life. This is what I was learning to do: I was learning to laugh through it all.

As Norman Cousins so aptly describes in his memoir, Anatomy of an Illness, humor is a powerful tool for recovery and maintenance of health. It became one of my most valuable strategies for staying afloat.

July 28, 2006

A break in the weather, a walk on the beach with a friend, some sleep, a session with my therapist, lots of email lectures from friends, and I feel better. Deloris is in pretty good shape, too, although less than absolutely steady these past couple of days. She was up most of the night (I was, too) going back and forth to the bathroom. I hope it is the condition-getting-worse-before-it-gets-better syndrome. Whenever she takes a nap, which is usually a couple of times a day, she wakes up, thinks it's morning and wants breakfast-muesli and fresh blueberries. I guess it could be worse. She also decided she would like to try going to the Senior Center a third day a week, which would give me another four to five hours of free time. I like it; it will make scheduling PT and other appointments a little tighter, but we can work it out.

I am also considering getting some nighttime help so that I can at least sleep through the night a couple times a week. I have some serious concerns and emotional hang-ups about doing that-we would not only be sleeping in separate beds, but on different floors; it seems like a step backward for Deloris, but perhaps a step toward increased self-care for me. And there is the thing about strangers in the house. I haven't talked with Deloris about it yet, although she is concerned that I am not sleeping well. I think I will gather information first. Don't know what the costs are.

Being a believer in the principles of Open Space and Angeles Arrien's Four-Fold Way, I have decided that several of these concepts are useful constructs for me to have in mind in my daily approach to the present situation. Specifically, accepting that whatever happens is the only thing that can happen and that I must be open to outcomes but not attached to a particular one. My therapist says that it is appropriate to be attached to Deloris's safety as an outcome. I think I am considering this from a much more macro, long-term perspective. And, in a funny sense, whichever Deloris shows up at any given time is the right Deloris. I don't know if the application is forced, but it feels like a useful approach for me to play with. Perhaps, it will make me more accepting and less directive when I know her safety is not at stake.

Deloris talked me into leaving her alone this afternoon for about a half hour; I had to go to the post office to mail in a passport renewal application, and she did not want to go. We talked about my concerns, and she promised to call 911 if she fell and could not get up. When I returned home, she was fine, still in the same place she had been when I left, having spent the time talking with friends on the phone. It's a start-baby steps, but steps nonetheless.

Allan

CHAPTER EIGHT
AS RELENTLESS AS THE
ROUND OF TIDES

The Princess and the Pee

DELORIS'S STROKE caused bladder problems, which adversely impacted our lifestyle. She spent an inordinate amount of time in bathrooms. Wherever we went, her first question when we arrived was, "May I use your bathroom?" It didn't matter whether our destination was ten minutes away or an hour. Her last stop before leaving home was the bathroom. It was always her first stop when we returned. Something needed to be done.

The first urologist we consulted diagnosed the problem as interstitial cystitis, a bladder inflammation of unknown origin, for which there is no known cure. While there were medications that might help alleviate some of the symptoms, most have unacceptable side effects, such as confusion and short-term memory loss, two conditions Deloris did not need to have exacerbated.

Some people with the condition are helped by dietary changes whose efficacy could not be predicted without actually making the changes. That meant eliminating foods that Deloris-and I-consider most desirable: all fruits and fruit juices (except blueberries and melons), tomatoes, coffee, wine, and spicy foods. Gone were Chinese, Thai, Mexican, and Korean cuisines. The deal breaker turned out to be no chocolate! Deloris and I both wondered if the potential cure wasn't worse than the affliction.

Deloris did, however, try both the diet and the medications, and neither helped her bladder problems. So, she ended her food restrictions and faced the continued urinary urgency with the consolation of knowing she could enjoy a cup of coffee, a glass of wine, Pad Thai, and chocolate.

One of the common symptoms of interstitial cystitis is pain, and Deloris was pain free. That made me question the accuracy of the diagnosis, which seemed to be one of last resort: when nothing else fit, interstitial cystitis was the default diagnosis. I became convinced Deloris's condition was something else-a condition for which a cure was possible. We decided to get a second opinion and consulted Dr. Kathleen Kobashi, the director of a urinary incontinence clinic in a major Seattle hospital. Her diagnosis was different indeed: a neurogenic hyperactive bladder condition.

Dr. Kobashi explained that neural pathways function as communication channels among body organs, including the bladder and brain. Through these, the bladder sends gotta pee messages to the brain, which replies hang on-now is not a good time or go ahead. Deloris's stroke had apparently disrupted these lines of communication, creating obstacles that prevented the hang on messages from being delivered. Dr. Kobashi was certified to work with an implant that circumvented the blocks and, through low-level electrical impulses, transmitted the hang on messages to the bladder.

Unfortunately, a test of the implant indicated it wasn't feasible for Deloris. Proper functioning of the implant depended on its accurate calibration. This, in turn, depended on feedback from the patient. Deloris's diminished executive functioning prevented her from providing this necessary data.

Remaining treatment options involved varying degrees of invasiveness. The least invasive, and most experimental, treatment involved injecting botulism toxin (Botox) directly into the bladder wall. Botox would cause the muscles to relax, easing the urgency response. The drug was expensive and neither it nor the injection procedure was covered by Deloris's insurance. While Medicare covered Botox for several non-cosmetic functions, a neurogenic hyperactive bladder was not one of them. Despite the financial concerns, we decided to try the treatment. Deloris's pharmacist brother would initially supply the drugs at his cost, while I prepared to challenge the denial of coverage.

I researched medical journals for studies supporting the use of Botox to treat hyperactive bladders. I was excited to have the intellectual challenge the appeal presented. If I employed my legal advocacy and academic research skills successfully and gained insurance coverage, I would be helping us and possibly other Medicare patients for whom Botox would become a viable and beneficial treatment. I submitted a four-page appeal which ultimately resulted in Deloris's HMO providing insurance coverage. We were thrilled, as was our doctor, at our victory against the insurance bureaucracy.

Tranquilizers failed to ease Deloris's nervousness on the day of the first treatment. A local anesthetic helped, but her anxiety and the perceived pain of the injections interfered with the protocol and made the procedure less than a success. We decided to try again, this time under general anesthesia, which was much easier on both doctor and patient. The results were more successful as well. The number and duration of Deloris's bathroom trips lessened; her sense of urgency and her incontinence eased dramatically. The psychological programming of staying close to a bathroom remained, but we trusted that would also ease with time.

When I quit smoking years before, I had been given back several hours a day. The hours I previously spent on smoking-related activities-buying cigarettes, looking for them, actually smoking, cleaning ashtrays, etc.-became available for other, more productive pursuits. Botox had a similar benefit for Deloris: she had more time and newfound freedom.

It's Actually a Loft

We bought our two-story Whidbey Island home, in 2002, after an extensive search, accepting we would have to move when it became impossible for one of us to climb stairs. We had looked for a house with only one floor but had found nothing we liked. I was originally ambivalent about the house, as it was more suburban in appearance than I envisioned for myself. Deloris loved it on first sight and after about ninety seconds of consultation with me, instructed our agent to get it for us.

Once I came to terms with my initial reluctance, we were both comfortable in the house. All the systems and appliances worked, a change from our older Seattle bungalow. I also appreciated the calming effect of the views and the quiet of the neighborhood.

The house was, however, ill designed for someone using a walker or wheelchair. Retrofitting for those purposes would be both inconvenient and expensive. I was concerned that remaining in the house was a dice throw, if not a time bomb. Other than the incident in the street, Deloris's falls, which were happening with more frequency, had not yet resulted in any serious injury. It seemed to me it was only a matter of time, however, before she would fall with devastating results. To lessen the potential harm from a fall, Deloris's physical therapist had suggested she either sleep on the floor or get a lower bed. Those ideas failed to consider her inability to get up and down from the floor or to climb the stairs.

The situation at home became acute one evening as we were getting ready to go to a friend's birthday party. Coming down the stairs from our second floor bedroom where she had changed clothes for the party, Deloris froze. She stood on a step, both hands clinging to the banister, a look of fear on her face. She said, "I can't go any farther."

"You have to, hon. You can't just stay here in the middle of the stairs. Let's take it one step at a time." I kept my tone encouraging.

"I can't. I don't have the strength." She sat down.

"Take your time. When you're ready, just scootch down on your tush one step at a time." I envisioned the 911 call I would have to make if I could not talk her down the stairs.

"Nine-one-one. What is your emergency?"

"My wife is stuck on the stairs and can't get down."

"I'm sorry. What did you say?"

"My wife is stuck walking down the stairs. She can't move. I can't lift her by myself. I need some help."

Stifling a snicker, the dispatcher says, "A unit is on its way."

I didn't make the call. More than an hour later, Deloris reached the bottom step. She was physically and emotionally exhausted; I was scared. I had to wonder what I would have done if this had happened when we didn't have the luxury of time to wait for Deloris to move. Or when she would be truly unable to get down the stairs.

On one hand, I wanted to be patient and research a solution to our housing situation. On the other hand, I had to act quickly. Yet-like Deloris on the stairs that night-I was frozen, unable to do anything; I simply couldn't make a decision. I struggled with how to solve a problem that seemed insoluble. It wasn't possible that within a couple of days I could sell our house and move us to another. We had no place to go, and I really didn't want to move. Nor could I remodel the house quickly. Some other solution was needed.

In an act based more on an acknowledgement of worst case scenarios than of present realities, I also explored the options of assisted living or a group home. I was not planning on "dropping Deloris off" at the home and returning to the Island; rather, I was looking into options where we could continue to live together and Deloris could get the accommodations and the help she needed now and in the future. To say I was depressed by the prospect and the exploratory ventures would be an understatement. I was not ready to move into an institutional environment, regardless of how nice they were or how many activities they provided. Neither of us, I believed, was ready to relinquish what freedom of movement and decision-making we retained. While Deloris's physical needs might have been better met in such a living situation, I doubted either of our emotional needs, or mental health, would thrive. At the same time, it was an option that required exploration. I was gathering information on alternatives which even if not presently needed may be sometime in the not too distant future.

As it became increasingly obvious that Deloris couldn't go up and down the stairs as easily as before, I asked her if she wanted to sleep downstairs. She already took afternoon naps on the daybed in the living room. If necessary, I thought, she could sleep in it at night as well. She said no. In truth, I was ambivalent about the proposal, knowing I would be uncomfortable sleeping on a different floor than Deloris. More important, I thought, despite the difficulty she had going up and down the stairs, she was safer with me sleeping beside her.

My body and mind were attuned to Deloris's smallest movements; I would be wide-awake within seconds whenever I sensed Deloris needed help. If Deloris slept on the first floor, there was no place for me to sleep next to her. Nor did I want to pay a caregiver to sit in a chair beside my wife in order to help her to and from the bathroom a couple of times a night. The stairs were not wide enough for a standard chair lift; a customized chair lift was too expensive. Major house renovations would take time, even if they were possible, practical, and affordable.

No option that involved staying in our present house seemed feasible. The clock was ticking, and it scared the hell out of me. I needed to fix the problem and had no idea how.

One evening Ben and Fredericka, who were back from New York, came over for dinner. As we were eating, I described my frustration and stress at being unable to come up with a workable living solution. Ben looked around the room. "Think of the downstairs as one big open space. You've been in our loft in New York. This has the same sort of possibilities. Move your bed downstairs, set up some screens, and live on one floor. It's what we do in New York."

I looked around and was surprised by what I saw. "That could work," I said.

While not ideal from a decorator's standpoint, the solution entailed minimal inconvenience. We would no longer have a functional living room, but it was a lot easier, and less expensive, than moving. And if we bought a new bed, we could move our present one into the empty room upstairs and have a real guest room.

As a teacher of critical thinking, I was familiar with how our strong feelings can cloud our thought processes. I had been caught up in my own emotional maelstrom and could neither recognize it for what it was nor find a means to escape it. I had needed another pair of eyes, someone uninvolved who could look at things dispassionately and come up with a rational, workable solution. Ben's suggestion excited me on several levels. We could remain in our home, and I would now have new material for my classes: a personal example of how a dispassionate party can help in problem solving.

With the help of friends to move furniture and the purchase of a new bed, Deloris and I began living on one floor. We had previously installed a shower in the laundry room when Kay was living with us. Combined with the powder room facilities, this gave Deloris full bathroom functionality, albeit a bit more crowded than upstairs. I converted our old bedroom into a sitting room, which I used to have some quiet space and privacy. My office remained on the first floor, which allowed me to work and be available to Deloris. Putting up some Japanese screens we had stored in the garage created privacy from people entering the front door. The arrangement would not make House Beautiful, but it was workable.

I Dread the Night

Deloris and I live beside the Salish Sea, which like all bodies of salt water, has daily tides. The time and size of each high and low tide varies in a regular rhythm throughout a monthly cycle. Deloris's and my life seemed to be in a similar ebb and flow but in a substantially more erratic pattern. Certain events, however, were almost certain to take place daily; some of these were more likely to happen in the daylight hours, others were nocturnal. In many ways, especially in the years immediately after Deloris's return home from the hospital, the nights were the hardest, if for no other reason than that the nighttime events were interruptions to my sleep. I always seemed to be tired.

Many nights, I dreaded going to bed. No matter how soundly Deloris was sleeping, as soon as I approached the bed, she was wide-awake, thinking it was time to get up. And she wanted to go to the bathroom, regardless of any identifiable physical or biological need. Her need postponed my bedtime by at least a half hour and often longer, as it took time for me to help her to get out of bed and over to the potty seat next to the bed. While not the most handsome piece of living room furniture, the potty seat (Deloris informed me commode is the proper term) seemed to fit in with the décor of a queen-sized bed (ours) and a single hospital bed (Deloris's daybed) in the same room. And it was easier for Deloris to use than going to the powder room down the hall.

I don't know why, but late night potty trips always took longer than daytime bathroom visits. I became easily frustrated when I was tired and wanted to go to sleep. While Deloris sat on the potty chair, however, all I could do was wait until she was finished so I could help her back to bed. I couldn't go to sleep, even though she encouraged me to do so. If I did, she might well sit on the potty seat for hours, as she did one night, when she awoke at 2:30 a.m. to go to the bathroom.

"Do you need help?" I asked one night, while still mostly asleep. Deloris was sitting on the side of the bed, gazing at the potty seat.

"No. I can do it."

I knew she was often capable of standing up and moving the foot or so to the potty seat, so I rolled over and went back to sleep. Several hours later I awoke to find her still sitting on the side of the bed, in the same position as I had left her earlier.

"Why are you still sitting there? Did you use the potty chair yet?"

"No. I was just sitting here, waiting to get up."

"Hunh!" I grunted, tossing the covers off my body. I struggled to my feet, walked around to where she sat, and helped her up and to the potty chair. I then went back to bed. Within minutes, she was finished, had gotten up, and joined me in bed. She, of course, fell right back to sleep. I remained awake for nearly an hour.

Then there were nights when, after sitting on the potty chair for thirty minutes or so, she wanted to talk. I love talking with Deloris; I just didn't want to do it at 1:00 a.m. when I needed sleep. I finally decided that if I programmed my mind to include a half-hour interlude between the time I got to bed until I was actually able to sleep, helping Deloris to make a middle-of-the-night potty run might be less frustrating. It would be part of my nightly routine, and talk might even be acceptable.

One night, I came to bed shortly after 1:00 a.m. As I approached the bed, Deloris said, "I can't believe I woke up to the sounds of grand opera coming from your office." She knew opera was not a musical form I enjoyed.

"It was actually Gilbert and Sullivan on TV. I was watching Linda Ronstadt and Kevin Kline in The Pirates of Penzance."

"That's one of my favorites. I was in it years ago with the Seattle Gilbert and Sullivan Society. How was it?"

"It was good. I liked it. Of course, I'm a Linda Ronstadt fan and I haven't seen any other production, so I am probably not a good critic."

Our conversation continued for ten or fifteen minutes while Deloris got up, used the potty chair, and returned to bed. It was fun, despite the time. Deloris was alert, aware of her surroundings and the topic of conversation, present in the moment. It was like the conversations we used to have. And she didn't dawdle on the potty chair. Maybe the key was to engage her in stimulating conversations so bodily functions happened automatically without her attention focused on them.

My patience was again tested several days later when I awoke about 3:30 a.m. and saw Deloris walking (I use that term in the most generic sense) to the bathroom. Sometimes, even though the potty seat was close by, she decided to walk the twenty-five feet or so to the bathroom. Surprised she had gotten as far as she had on her own, I saw she was not stable enough to make it all the way without assistance. I sprang out of bed to help her and my presence triggered a common middle-of-the-night discussion about how it was too early to get dressed or eat breakfast. She was considerably more awake than I was and voiced a desire to stay that way.

"It's the middle of the night. You need to go back to bed."

"I'm awake. I need to get dressed."

After several rounds of this exchange, with my voice increasing in volume along with my frustration level, I reached my limit. I yelled, "Go to bed. I am really damned tired of going through this every night. You wake up in the middle of night and want to stay up. That's not going to happen. You need to go back to bed!"

"No, I don't."

"Yes, you do. We're both going back to bed."

My anger began to ebb and I saw how controlling I was being. This was partly due to my exhaustion and partially out of concern for Deloris's safety. I didn't want to stay up, and I didn't think she could be up alone safely. I took a deep breath, centered myself, and took a different approach.

"Look. I am exhausted and I have to get some sleep."

"So, go back to bed," she said.

"I'm not comfortable with you being up and about if I am in bed. I'm worried something might happen and you'll hurt yourself. So, if you're up, I have to be. And I really don't want to be. So, come to bed."

"I understand. But I'm okay being up by myself. Nothing is going to happen. Go back to bed. I'll be there shortly."

I gave up, too tired to argue, and went back to bed.

Twenty minutes later, I was still alone in bed. I got up and returned to the bathroom. I found Deloris sitting on the toilet, reading a magazine, comfortable in her "library," the water running in the sink as she waited for it to warm up so she could wash her face. She was preparing to dress and have breakfast.

Tired, frustrated, and upset, I said, "Get up and go back to bed," and then walked away, attempting to control my emotions. A few minutes later, I returned and helped her to her feet. She stood, hunched over, her hands grasping the grab bar, her head touching the wall, unable or unwilling to move.

"Stand up." I tried to be encouraging.

"Okay."

"Hold your head up. Straighten your back."

"Okay." She was mumbling now.

My coaching triggered no movement. It seldom did when she got stuck like this. It was as if no connection existed between her brain and her legs. As I realized the futility of my words, I had the image of the two of us standing in this position night after night after night after night after night . . . with no end or progress in sight. I lost it.

"Stand up straight, dammit!" My voice hit a totally inappropriate volume. I figured the louder I spoke and more insistent I was, the more likely Deloris's brain would hear and transmit the appropriate message to her legs, which would then move. The reality, of course, was something else. Deloris heard my raised voice and resented my yelling at her. I walked away again, this time to hide my tears. I was exhausted, frustrated, and upset with myself for yelling.

When I finally got her back to bed, almost an hour after this episode began, I lay in the darkness, holding her in my arms, hoping I was able to hide from her my tears and quiet sobs. I may have succeeded in protecting Deloris, but I couldn't shield myself from the painful sense of futility. I was overwhelmed by the thought that this was as good as our life together was going to be for the foreseeable future. I finally fell asleep, some time after she did.

I was beginning to understand the foundations of verbal and psychological abuse and the realization scared the hell out of me. I did not perceive of myself as an abuser. Was there another explanation for my actions? Was there a label less emotionally loaded I could apply? While there is no justification for abuse, no matter the nature, there were triggers which could be identified. Perhaps being sleep deprived was one reason I found myself losing patience almost daily. Some of my reactions were motived by fear. Deloris's falls almost always put me over the edge. I visualized her unable to get up, having broken a hip or with blood streaming from a crack in her head. The memory of her sitting in the entryway that dark January morning several years before, her face covered with blood, was never far from my mind's eye. Yet that midwinter excursion to the mailbox was the only time she had really hurt herself when she fell. So, looking back now, I have to acknowledge that my fear that Deloris would be hurt was only a part of my response. I had other fears as well, and staying free of these had long required me to be alert, to have my rational mind as well as all my senses operating efficiently.

For over twenty years I was a criminal defense attorney. Throughout that time people's lives, or at least their freedom for years to come, might depend on my being alert and awake, able to respond quickly to what was happening in the courtroom. I had to be able to discern meaning in a person's tone of voice, body language, the words being used, whether by the judge, the prosecutor, a witness, or my client. My mental acuity was a tool I saw as vital. It was something I'd needed once to succeed professionally, something I needed now to protect my wife, something that was basic to my being me-and it was being seriously compromised by my inability to sleep. At some subconscious level I knew this and I blamed Deloris, or at least her condition, for the loss of something I found to be essential.

Daytime brought its own rhythm and concerns. Some were variations on the same themes that played out at night; others were unique to the day.

No More Migraines, But . . .

An inability to comply with my sense of appropriate time was only one issue we confronted. Deloris had been plagued by migraines several times a month before her stroke, but had not suffered one since. That was the good news. The not-so-good news was in their stead she now experienced the spontaneous projectile vomiting, increased falls, joint pain, and general feeling of malaise. Also, the getting stuck that had preceded moving our bed into the living room started to occur more often. It didn't happen only on the stairs; it came up sometimes when Deloris was in the shower, when she was walking across a room in the house, when she was in the yard, or away from the house altogether. Everything would be fine; she would be moving as well as she always did; and then for no discernible reason, she would stop. When that happened, I often became irrationally angry and started yelling at her, as if the volume of my voice would force the desired movement. Of course, the actual reaction was different, with Deloris saying, "Quit yelling at me. It won't help, and I don't like it. Yelling at me won't work. I don't like being like this any more than you do. In fact, I like it even less."

Once again, I was chastened, forced by her words to realize I was interacting with this intelligent, beautiful, vibrant adult woman I loved as if she were a recalcitrant, stubborn child. More than once I told her, "You know, if I was the one being treated the way I am treating you, I would have killed me a long time ago. Thank you for being so patient and understanding." Deloris is writing a murder mystery now in which a woman's husband is brutally killed; perhaps it's her outlet.

I tried a new approach, offering suggestions rather than issuing commands.

"What are you feeling?" I asked, attempting to discern what was happening in her body.

"My legs feel dead."

"Talk to your feet. Tell your right foot what you want it to do. Maybe it isn't listening to the messages the brain is sending it."

"Okay. Right foot-move six inches to the left."

Nothing.

"Right foot. Can you hear me? Please move a bit to the left."

Still nothing.

"Can you move them at all?" I asked.

"No."

"Can you try?"

"I am."

"Try harder." What can I say? That was what came out. As the words left my mouth, I realized how ridiculous and unhelpful I was being.

I didn't know what to do in these situations, other than to leave Deloris alone and let her work through it. Acceptance and satisfaction were apparently not my style, although I very much wanted them to be. I knew Deloris's pain was real, and her inability to move was obvious.

I had been seduced by her previous mobility, convinced she had reached a new plateau. I had forgotten that the post-stroke journey is one of fits and starts, ebbs and flows.

On one level I did know Deloris would get better on her own timeline, and nothing I desired or demanded could change that. There were, however, more times than I care to remember when my expectations fueled an overreaction to what was truly normal behavior.

In retrospect, I think it may have been a control issue. Lawyers love to be in control; it's what we are trained to do. Uncertainty, especially in a trial, is unacceptable. You don't ask questions you don't know the answers to; you do all you can to control the flow of the trial-the way in which a story is told, the facts that come out. You want your opponent to be compliant, to do what you expect. Order is inherent in our adversarial system of justice. Suddenly, my wife's foot was my adversary and I was unable to reason with it, to find a way to get it to act as I wanted. When this happened, I would become incensed. It was as if I was temporarily insane-even when I could see the situation arising. Perhaps especially when I could. It was as if the Evil Twin who lived inside me took over.

Deloris asked me to make an appointment for her with a new hairdresser she wanted to try. When I picked her up after her haircut, she had to climb down six steps to get to the parking area. She'd had no trouble getting up the stairs and into the salon. Coming down, however, was a different story.

There was a ramp out the back door, which might have been easier to navigate but required a bit more walking. Deloris opted for the stairs. "I don't want to use the ramp. I would rather climb down the stairs." This surprised me, given her recent incidents of freezing and the fact that she always had more trouble going down stairs than up them.

She went down the first three steps with no problem. Then she froze. Minutes passed as she stood, knees bent, hunched over, her hands gripping both her cane and my arm, almost cutting off my circulation.

I struggled to keep my balance, and hers. "Can you move your leg?"

Nothing.

"Okay, now, pick up your right foot and move it down six inches." Still no response.

"Tell your leg it has to move. You can't spend the rest of your life on this step." The leg ignored the message.

Nothing I could say or do enticed her to move. It was hot. We were both tired and getting cranky. I knew the position she was in would cause her a great deal of pain unless she moved. "Hang on to me," I suggested. "I am going to pick up your leg and move it. We have to get down these stairs."

"Okay." She was acquiescent, if a bit worried. I held onto her, picked up her leg mid-thigh, and moved it to the next lower step. That broke the spell. She was able to move down the final steps and into the car. Both of us were spent by the physical and emotional energies this short journey required.

On one occasion, Deloris was half out of the shower when she stopped moving. One leg was firmly planted, the other less so. She was shivering from being cold and was able to stand only because she had a tight grip on my hand. Once again, she had frozen in place.

"Can you move?"

"No."

"Pick up your right leg."

"It doesn't want to cooperate."

"Talk to it; ask it to do what you want."

"Please take a step. I need to get out of the shower." Her leg ignored the request.

"Deloris's leg," I addressed. "Lift up from the floor and move six inches forward." I too was ignored.

"Did you hear what I said, Leg?" My voice increased in volume and emotion. "Move!" Time passed without response. "Move. Dammit," I screamed. "You need to get out of the shower. Now, get the fuck in motion."

Her leg ignored me. The rest of Deloris attempted to do so as well.

Some part of my mind obviously thought that yelling profanities-language and a decibel level I had almost never used around Deloris before her stroke, but which erupted from me more and more often since-was going to break through the blocks in her neurological system and trigger movement. Intellectually, I knew that was not going to happen. Yet, when faced with Deloris's inability to move, I became irrational. I hated myself for it afterward, but in the crucial moment my response continued to be rage. I knew Deloris didn't appreciate my outbursts; hell, neither did I.

While others may disagree, as I look back, I considered my inability to control my anger a little like Deloris's inability to control parts of her body-the very situation that seemed to aggravate the anger. In both cases, a synapse wasn't firing in the right way. Somewhere between my brain and my mouth, the don't say that, you fool! message was lost. Deloris apparently experienced a similar breakdown along the neural pathways between her brain and other parts of her body. Her legs refused to do what the brain wanted them to, and nothing either one of us said or did could motivate that movement. Whether or not I was yelling at her, Deloris would stand, statue-like, frozen in place from the waist down, knees bent, shoulders hunched, head bowed, looking at her feet. Eventually, sometimes in a few minutes, sometimes up to twenty minutes later, Deloris's feet starting working and she was able to move once again.

Deloris's neurologist was not overly concerned about her freezing episodes. He suggested getting a CAT scan to see if there had been any noticeable change in her condition. The images showed no major changes. While no identifiable cause for her inactions could be determined, the scan showed no signs of Parkinson's, Alzheimer's, or other conditions about which we needed to be concerned.

While there was much to be thankful for, I was greatly disturbed by my reactions and the language I used in dealing with these situations. I had always thought of myself as being calm, accepting, compassionate. Yet, screaming obscenities at my wife, the woman I loved and was caring for, was the exact direct opposite of my self-image. Where was that anger coming from? It's true that I was required to be confrontational in the adversarial relationships when I was practicing law. Trials are zero-sum games: one person's loss is precisely his opponent's gain; a person either wins or loses. Yet even then, whatever anger I expressed in legal negotiations or the courtroom was for effect. It was not a manifestation of what I was feeling.

There had been some incidents much earlier in my life when I had expressed, and also felt, strong anger. Then, as now, my anger was directed at a person close to me. Thinking about it, I could see that what had truly angered and frustrated me weren't the actions, or inactions, of the other person but the inherent difficulties of the situation we were in.

What was happening right now with my wife was somewhat different. Even though I didn't think I was truly angry with Deloris, she received the brunt of my emotional outbursts. They were directed specifically at her-and at a time in her life when she was the least able to deal with them. Even as I screamed at her, and certainly immediately thereafter, I felt awful about what I was doing. Yet I could not seem to control myself, and this lack of control disturbed me at least as much as the actions themselves did. I needed to develop better control mechanisms and more productive responses to Deloris's various problems and behaviors. How was I going to do that?

Once again, as has happened so many times in our relationship, Deloris was my teacher. That she was probably not aware of the lesson she was providing made it all the more powerful.

In Her Own Time

About a year after returning home, Deloris had rejoined a writing class she had attended before her stroke. The instructor and her classmates were happy to have her back with them and looked forward to her contributions. The class was held in a church classroom about ten minutes from our house. I agreed to drop her off, entertain myself for the two hours of her class, and pick her up to go home. The problem lay in getting her ready and out of the house in time for the class.

Why did I care so much about her getting to class on time when she, apparently, did not? Was it about the impact on the others? The violation of my sense of what was right and polite? Perhaps it was the loss of my free time I found frustrating. Perhaps I was concerned about a lack of improvement in Deloris's condition or what I perceived to be attempts on her part to gain control and independence by setting our pace. Or perhaps when she was late, I felt it reflected poorly on me and my caregiving skills.

Here I should note my own tendency to operate on what's known locally by the affectionate term island time. I haven't worn a watch for years. I was seldom, if ever, on time for my appointments. But Deloris's schedule was another story. I felt her involvement in the writing class made it incumbent on me to ensure she showed up on time. This was what I told myself-even though I knew others didn't see it that way. Deloris's teacher and fellow students were happy she had returned to class and easily accommodated her needs and sense of time. So, why couldn't I?

Each Wednesday morning, I woke Deloris in plenty of time to do her morning ablutions, dress, have breakfast, and get to class. When I thought it was time to leave the house and Deloris wasn't ready to go, I became first frustrated and then angry.

"We have to leave in ten minutes. Hurry up."

"Why the hell do you need to go to the bathroom? You were just in there ten minutes ago!"

"Come on, damn it. You don't have all day."

Once we were finally driving to class, I would often use the time to apologize and attempt to reason with her, explaining that all I wanted to do was get her to class on time, so she could honor her commitments to her teacher and classmates. "I know you can do it," I would say. "Why can you be ready when Paratransit comes to pick you up, but you can't, or won't, do that for me?"

This was not entirely accurate; I was conveniently forgetting that the Paratransit driver often had to wait for Deloris to be ready. Like any good politician or lawyer, I would spin the facts to fit my own story-my wife was late because, with me, she thought she could get away with it.

Negotiation based on logic and rationality was what I had been trained to do and comprised much of what I did and taught in my profession. I thought I was calming myself after my outbursts of anger. In retrospect, I can see that I was reassuring myself of the correctness of my position. I say this because immediately after I made these arguments to Deloris, I usually resorted to ultimatums: "If you can't get ready in time for me to get you to class on time, you can make your own arrangements. I've had it."

It was a paradox. I wanted to support Deloris's engaging in activities that gave greater meaning to her life, allowing her to feel at least partly like the woman she was before the stroke. At the same time, I seemed unable to let things happen at their own pace, unable to let go of my own sense of appropriate timing. As I've mentioned, I suspected Deloris was adopting a passive-aggressive approach to my demands, intentionally slowing her actions to demonstrate a sense of independence and resentment.

One morning when I had reached the end of my patience, Deloris brought home to me the necessity of my achieving some buoyancy and acceptance.

"You are doing this just to piss me off," I yelled at her, my face red with fury. "Get out of the fucking bathroom and into the car. You have to be to class in ten minutes."

Deloris looked at me with incredulity. "Why are you talking to me like this?" she said. "I am not your enemy."

Her words stunned me. She had held up a mirror to me, and the impact on me was like a physical shock. I am not your enemy. Of course she wasn't. Then why was I acting like she was? The self I saw reflected back in Deloris's words was dark and angry, unlike a man professing to love the person to whom he was talking. I didn't like that dark, angry self. Deloris's ability to make me see this unpleasant image made me appreciate and love her even more. My task was to change my behavior to fit these feelings.

I took a deep breath, apologized, and walked away, leaving her to get ready for class in her own time.

Later, when I reflected on our behaviors, I marveled at Deloris's ability to allow my anger to wash over her as she looked beneath it to the pain and loss I was feeling. Her ability and willingness to not respond in kind made me realize what an incredible teacher she is and what amazing opportunities for life lessons I am being given.

How could I hold that realization in the midst of our daily routines? Floating sometimes seemed impossible.

April 13, 2007

Yesterday was the day! Botox injections finally took place. We had discussed one or two vials (either dose, according to the latest research, is equally effective; more just lasts longer.) While we had theoretically decided to use two vials, postponing the next visit, Deloris changed her mind as the needle was being inserted, and inserted, and inserted . . . She was very sensitive and did not like being stuck! Who does? Each dose involves 10 injections of 10 milliliters each, in various parts of the bladder. Not counting prep work, the procedure took maybe ten minutes-two urologists (Dr. Kobashi who is Dee's doctor, and another one who assisted) and one RN, with me holding Dee's hand and reminding her to breathe! The medical staff was pleasant, actually cracking jokes with Dee and me as the prep and procedure was taking place.

The pain was gone as soon as the syringe was removed. There was little recovery time needed-merely the promise of Ben and Jerry's ice cream and a stop at University Village for some shopping. Deloris did really well! And Dr. Kobashi was pleased with Group Health's decision to cover the procedure. Both she and the entire urology department had been strong advocates for insurance coverage, as they believed in the medical efficacy of the procedure. The doctor complimented me, again, on the quality of the appeal statement I put together and the research it included. Guess I learned something in law school!

So, now we wait to see if the shots were effective. Kobashi said that for some people the effects are immediate; for others it may take a couple of days or up to two weeks. The only downside concern was the possibility of retention, so I was shown how to insert a catheter. The joys of being a lifelong learner! Given Deloris's actions and reactions, it is pretty clear to me this is knowledge I will not have to apply, at least not this week. I haven't noticed any change in her condition, although she reports feeling a slight reduction in urgency. If that keeps up . . .

Tomorrow is the Welcome the Whales parade in downtown Langley. Whales, I think, are the only tourists that all of Whidbey Island enjoys having visit. They don't spend any money, but they also don't clog up the ferry line. The parade should be fun-it lasts maybe fifteen minutes. People have been seeing whales already this season so, who knows, maybe one will show up. Deloris is moving pretty well and often feeling like she has some energy and wants to do things. So, if the weather permits and we are both moving well, I think we'll go to the parade.

Allan

CHAPTER NINE
AMOR FATI: LOVE WHAT IS

All I Want for Hanukkah Is My Car Keys

> *You asked what I want for Hanukkah, and the answer is I want the keys to my car, and for you to treat me as an adult, and allow me to make my own decisions and be responsible for myself.*
>
> *I know you doubt that I am yet capable of it, and you are afraid I will hurt myself. I think you can deal with your fear if you allow me the chance to demonstrate that I am capable of more than you think.*
>
> *I also know that you are compassionate and can probably understand that there are pains beyond that of falling down-such as being declared incompetent. Surely we can come to some compromise on this that will satisfy us both.*

I SMILED as I read the note Deloris had written and left for me on the kitchen table. Its wording, and the tone Deloris had used, touched me. Yet I knew I could not give her the gift she wanted. While a number of issues set me off, Deloris asking to drive never bothered me. Perhaps it was because I thought she knew driving was beyond her present abilities-although she continually raised the issue. We live in hope.

This stalemate was broken a few months later when Deloris needed a routine MRI done. We made our usual preparations for a trip to the mainland clinic where the procedure was to be administered. We put a cooler packed with blue ice in the trunk for stops at Costco and Trader Joe's, discussed where to eat in Seattle, and loaded up some snacks. I put my laptop in the car so I could work while Deloris was being scanned. A trip off-island took organization and often involved taking more stuff than my immigrant grandparents brought with them when they came to America.

The MRI scan and its preparation usually took several hours. Deloris had been gone for nearly three hours and I was just beginning to worry when a young woman in a white coat approached, introduced herself as a doctor, and asked, "Have you been told what happened?"

My heart stopped. All sorts of images flowed through my mind, none of them welcome or happy. "Uh, no."

"Your wife had a seizure while she was being prepped for the MRI. I wasn't in the room, but the nurse said it was minor. Apparently, when she was being given a sedative injection, your wife started clenching her fists. She had tremors in her arms and legs and may have lost consciousness for a few seconds. She was given something to relax her, and after she calmed down, the MRI continued. We've contacted her neurologist, and anti-seizure meds have been prescribed. We're going to transfer her to the walk-in clinic to monitor her for a while."

I understood the words I was hearing, but what did this mean about Deloris's condition?

An hour later I was allowed to see her. Tubes ran from her nostrils to a nearby oxygen tank. She was conscious, alert, yet somewhat tired. Her hands and toes were twitching, while her head moved from side to side. It was the same behavior she had exhibited earlier while in the hospital. Then, and now, her care providers were concerned but displayed no sense of urgency. Apparently I was the only one feeling panic. Of course, I was the only one who had a personal relationship with Deloris. I was the one who lived with her.

Deloris didn't know she had experienced any trouble nor had any memory of her seizure. She was aware of the twitching and tremors but had no idea why any of this was happening.

"I think the person giving me an injection was not very good," she said. "I'm not sure she knew what she was doing. She couldn't find a vein and stuck me several times. It hurt."

Maybe Deloris had reacted to the injection or the difficulties with the needle; maybe it was low blood sugar. I hoped the seizure was not serious, and at the same time I was aware the cause might never be known. The MRI results and Deloris's response to her new medication were what mattered most.

The neurologist said neither the MRI scans nor today's seizure indicated new concerns and released Deloris to return home. I considered this a good sign. Nevertheless, the visions going through my mind were nothing I wanted to have happen. I remained hypervigilant.

The only medical consequence of her seizure was a pricey medication Deloris was to take twice a day for the foreseeable future. If the medication worked, she would suffer no further seizures. That was the only test of its efficacy.

I was reminded of an old Groucho Marx routine when he was asked why he was always snapping his fingers. "I do it to keep the elephants away."

"But there are no elephants for hundreds of miles," his colleague says.

"See, it works!"

The new medication initially turned Deloris into a stumbling, mumbling automaton. In this condition, she fell several more times. The noise of her hitting the ground, while becoming a bit more common, always filled me with apprehension. Luckily, the only thing she ever injured was her pride. And once the proper dosage was determined, her stability and lucidity returned.

Another consequence of Deloris's seizure was that it changed our discussion on her driving. Washington State does not allow anyone who has suffered a seizure to drive until they have been seizure-free for some time. This episode made it legally impossible for Deloris to drive for the immediate future-and relieved me from being the bad guy and taking her car keys away.

"Why can't I drive myself?" Deloris asked, several months after the seizure. "I've been driving myself for almost fifty years. I know how to drive."

"Right, but that was before your stroke and before the seizure. Now the state won't let you drive until a doctor says it's okay. You know that."

"Yeah, I know."

Deloris had been told this by her neurologist and understood the reason. She understood it as well as she was capable of making those sorts of connections. Whenever we were at the doctor's however, she would ask, "When do you think I can start driving?"

"I'm not sure it is such a good idea," the neurologist would say. "Let's wait a bit longer. I am not ready to sign off on the certificate."

I didn't file anything with Washington State about Deloris's seizure, but the hospital apparently did since Deloris received a formal notice saying her driving privileges were suspended. It also specified that state regulations prohibit a person from driving until that person has been seizure-free for twelve months.

Fifteen months after her seizure, Deloris started asking again when she would be able to drive.

"Can you get to the car by yourself, open the door, get in, and remember how to get to where you are going?" I asked.

"I've always done so in the past."

"Sure. But have you done it recently?"

"Well, no. But I can."

"I will be happy to talk about you driving when you are able to walk out the door, through the garage, and get into the car by yourself. Until then, relax and enjoy having a chauffeur."

In America, the inability to drive is one of the most potent manifestations of a lack of independence. To have been mobile all your adult life and suddenly be deprived of car keys, to be unable to go anywhere on your own, to be reliant on another person's availability and willingness to drive is the epitome of dependence. We have an excellent, and free, bus service on Whidbey Island and a paratransit service for the disabled that would pick Deloris up and drop her off at our front door on the days she went to the Senior Center or elsewhere. While convenient, Deloris did not consider it the same as being able to drive.

On the other hand, the thought of Deloris driving, alone, or worse, with me in the car, scared the hell out of me. When we were in the car together, she was always convinced we were heading in the wrong direction. Deloris's physical condition and limited mobility made it impossible for her to get to and into the car by herself. Her cognitive issues made the ability to remember where the car was parked questionable at best. I knew that driving was not an option for her.

The University of Washington School of Medicine had a driver-training program for people who had suffered strokes or brain injuries. It was expensive and required referral by a physician. I told Deloris about it and said I was comfortable with her driving if she passed the course. Whether I would be willing to get in the car with her behind the wheel was another matter. Until that time, however, I would take her where she needed to go. And she would have to convince her doctor to give her a referral for the training program, something she had not yet succeeded in doing.

As Deloris's birthday approached, it was time to renew her driver's license. The closest place to do so was in Oak Harbor, about fifty minutes from our home. We decided to combine the trip with some shopping and dinner.

We arrived at the Department of Licensing office shortly before closing time. I pushed open the door with my butt as I backed Deloris's wheel chair into the room. We took a number and waited our turn.

"How long have you been in the wheelchair," the DOL employee asked Deloris.

"About ten minutes," she responded. He was not amused.

"You're going to have to take a drivers' test before I can issue a renewal of your license."

"No problem," Deloris said. "It's been several years since I had my seizure."

"Seizure." he said. It wasn't a question. "I don't have any record of that. If you had a seizure, you will need a doctor's statement verifying your ability to drive, even before you take the test. Do you have one?"

We did not, of course. Nor did I think we would be able to get one. If Deloris didn't have a license, driving would not be an issue. "Why don't you just get an ID card now? That way you'll be able to cash checks, get through airport security, and do all those other things you need ID for," I said. "When you're ready to drive, we will get the doctor's referral, come back here, and you can take the test."

Deloris agreed and posed for the requisite photo. We then left the office and I drove to a Mexican restaurant where we toasted her new ID card with margaritas.

I Read About It in a Mystery Novel

Sometimes an Aha! moment occurs in the strangest place. One day while pedaling a stationary bike at the gym, I was listening to a detective story on my iPod. One of the characters was a neuropsychologist who tested patients to determine the extent of their cognitive abilities. I had never heard of this specialization before, but immediately I knew it was what I needed to help me come to terms with Deloris's diminished capabilities. Deloris had accepted not driving; could I accept it-could I accept the hundreds of ways my beloved wife was not functioning as she once had? I felt certain that if neurological tests told me Deloris had cognitive ability limitations, I would be able to accept those limitations as fact. This recognition would make life infinitely easier. I would no longer demand more from my wife than she was capable of doing. Here, at last, was a practical way to address my ongoing anger!

Deloris's HMO had neuropsychologists on contract, and she agreed to see one. Her current neurologist was less than excited by my desire to bring this new specialist into Deloris's care cadre. He thought the results from this kind of testing would not provide useful information. He believed her behavior could be the result of some mini-seizures or ongoing (and as yet undiagnosed) neurological issues. I appreciated his input; however, as Deloris's medical advocate, I made decisions regarding her treatment based on my analysis of medical recommendations and information and not only because her doctor wanted to do, or not do something. I believed Deloris's progress depended in large measure on having her care providers do what we wanted done, regardless of their personal or institutional preferences. That is not to say I disregarded their professional recommendations or advice; rather, I factored them into consideration along with my own research.

I encouraged Deloris to see the neuropsychologist because of my own desire to obtain additional objective verification of her condition. I had a feeling my expectations of Deloris were unrealistic, but that wasn't enough to allow me to let go of them. And if they were unrealistic I wanted to let go of those expectations. I didn't explain this to Deloris, but I saw her neuropsychological testing as a procedure for my benefit. It was necessary for my treatment, not hers.

Exploration into brain functioning and its role in human behavior has a long history. Contemporary neuropsychology developed, in part, to treat military personnel returning from war zones. It is also a useful diagnostic tool for individuals suffering head trauma from stroke, concussion, accidents, athletics, or other causes. What most intrigued me was neuroscience's diagnostic function.

Deloris and I journeyed into Seattle to see this neuropsychologist and his assistant. The battery of tests he proposed took about eight hours. These tests are usually administered in two sessions. Since

Deloris's ability to focus and her optimal energy level usually lasted no more than a couple of hours, we decided to spread the tests out over at least four appointments. During testing, I was not allowed in the room, so my knowledge of what Deloris had to do is secondhand. Basically, her memory, hand-eye coordination and dexterity, recall, executive functioning (problem solving, follow-through, initiation,) and other skills were assessed and evaluated. The result was a set of baselines for what Deloris was neurologically and cognitively capable of doing.

Deloris handled the testing without difficulty, aside from becoming extremely tired. I spent a good part of the time eating corned beef sandwiches from a nearby market known for having Seattle's best corned beef. Other times I sat in the lobby or on the outside patio, grading papers or watching the passing urban scene.

The test results provided what I'd hoped they would: empirical data about the limits of Deloris's capabilities. I had not received this level of specificity from her neurologist, and getting it now helped me discard my notion that Deloris had greater physical capabilities than she was displaying. As I've said, I had sort of known, but had never emotionally accepted, the possibility that neurological blocks inhibited the proper transmission of messages allowing my wife to function. The test results confirmed this was so: Deloris was doing the best she could at this point in time. In all areas of functioning, more progress was possible, and even probable.

So, nothing new was contained in the information provided by the neuropsychologist. Yet the professional imprimatur placed on the data as a result of statistically validated testing allowed me to accurately interpret what I had previously seen and experienced. I might wish that my wife could function at a higher level. I might pray she would be able to. I could not, however, expect her to do more than she was capable of. To do so not only set her up to fail but triggered a response in me that made life hell for us both.

As I integrated this new knowledge, my anger and frustration dissipated. I was able to accept Deloris's limitations and abilities as shown in the neuropsychological test results as reality. I was happy to encourage Deloris to proceed at her own pace, offer whatever help and assistance she might need or want, and stop demanding she meet my expectations. This shift in my attitude made a tremendous difference in our lives.

The neurologist was concerned Deloris might be experiencing multiple, undetected mini-seizures that impacted her ability to focus and her energy level. He also considered these might be the cause of her freezing-in-place incidents and perhaps the periodic auditory and visual hallucinations she reported having. He wanted Deloris to undergo a multi-day, continually monitored EEG test. The good news was the tests showed Deloris had had no seizures. She also tested negative for blood clots in her legs, which were thought a possible cause of pain she was experiencing. The not-so-good news was that after Deloris spent five days lying in a hospital bed, tethered by monitoring wires attached at one end to electrodes glued to her scalp and the other end hooked to instruments connected to the wall, we had no more idea what was causing her problems than we had before. Deloris had, however, lost considerable strength and mobility, during her bed-stay, necessitating a transfer to intensive inpatient rehab before being released to return home.

When I visited her several days after the transfer, she was in bed, her still-tangled hair clotted with remnants of the glue that had held the EEG electrodes in place. Small red splotches marked the earlier connection locations. A chocolate brown shawl was draped across her shoulders.

She was asleep when I came in, so I changed the channel on the television in the corner of the room. It was the first thing Deloris noticed when she woke up. "This doesn't look like the Food Channel," she said. "What's going on?"

"You were asleep when I came in. I turned on the ball game."

"Well, I'm awake now. So please give me the remote." She held out her hand.

I did as she asked. She was the patient, and it was her room.

After finding something she wanted to watch, Deloris said, "I want to go home. I don't think anything in the contract I signed requires me to stay here." She handed me the admission agreement form with its standard boilerplate verbiage. "We can leave whenever I want."

"You're right. The contract does not require you to stay here. However, the doctor wants you to have some intensive therapy so you will get stronger," I responded.

"They'll be sorry. If I get strong, I'll kick their butts."

"That should be fun to watch."

If her banter was any indication, she'd almost returned to what passed for normal in those days. She was also talking more about her condition and how it felt. She summarized it one day, saying, "I really don't recommend a stroke to anyone, even though I haven't had any migraines since mine."

"My short-term memory has disappeared, so I have to keep being reminded if I am going to remember anything."

"My long-term memory is pretty good, so I remember a lot of things from the period before the stroke-my journalism career, the art and artists, my writing, those sorts of things. But I often have trouble remembering what happened this morning or yesterday."

"Physically, it's easier to take a step with my right foot. My left foot doesn't seem to get a clear signal from me."

That seemed a pretty accurate description of Deloris's condition. What she referred to as short-term memory was sometimes quantified in terms of minutes. Often, she would ask me a question, I'd answer, and five minutes later she'd ask the same question again. She was unable to remember or mentally retrieve my previous answer. The pattern was frustrating, but I knew she was struggling to make sense of her world. I was clear about one thing: my job was to help. After she had been in the rehab unit for about a week, the attending physician came into her room and asked Deloris how she felt.

"Exhausted," she said. "And my leg and back hurt."

"How long have you been feeling this way?"

"I don't remember. I think forever."

Smiling, the doctor did a quick exam. "Has anyone suggested a prescription for Ritalin?" she asked. "It may help you focus and give you some energy."

The week before I had watched an episode of Boston Legal in which a woman whose admission to Harvard Law School was revoked when the admissions office learned she had taken Ritalin prior to her entrance exams. Apparently, the drug, usually prescribed to treat hyperactive children, was popular on college campuses as a performance enhancer. It achieved this objective by increasing the user's energy level and ability to focus on the task at hand.

I immediately agreed and encouraged Deloris to try this new (to her) drug. If it worked as we hoped, it would help her operate at a higher level, gaining more results from her exercises and greater skill in her daily activities. I was elated that this might be the next step in Deloris's recovery. I had accepted that she was doing the best she could, but the prospect of her getting some assistance to enhance her abilities and allow her to recover more quickly thrilled me. Perhaps Ritalin was the answer, and I could have more of my wife back.

Shortly after starting small doses of a generic form of the drug, Deloris was able to engage fully and more completely in her physical therapy and training. Her mobility and independence increased, as did her ability to focus. She became a more nearly whole person, and I became a true believer in the medication, not to mention in the potential educational value of watching network television dramas.

I continually tell my students, "Everything is a learning opportunity."

When I say this, I'm not thinking of TV series and mystery novels as being prime catalysts for learning. Yet here they were-two breakthrough pieces of information first gleaned from those unexpected sources. Because I learned about neuropsychology in a mystery novel, we had been able to gauge Deloris's abilities and I had been able to accept her limitations. Because I learned about a certain medication on a television show, I had accepted a doctor's suggestion that Deloris use it-and that medication was a turning point in improving her ability to function. Had I not watched TV that night, I might not have been amenable to Deloris's trying another drug.

From the first days after Deloris's stroke, I began researching her condition and possible treatments. This has always been my method to learn something new: I seek to amass information and data. Now I see that everything is an opportunity to learn, every instance is a potential source of information. I suppose an openness to learn from whatever is available requires an acceptance of the present reality-the very essence of floating.

What Would Make You Happy?

I understood being the perfect caregiver was not necessary, or even possible. Nor was it a role I had ever come close to fulfilling. I accepted that being caring, alert, and considerate was more than sufficient. I had also begun to accept the long-term reality that Deloris would probably never return to her pre-stroke self. In order to care for her over this long and indeterminate time, I had to take care of myself. She and I were striving to develop a new normal, a life we could share and enjoy given the limitations imposed by her condition and my responsibilities.

As months became years, Deloris's condition progressed, plateaued, at times regressed, and progressed some more. As the Ritalin took effect, she became increasingly more capable of independent action. This allowed me to suggest outings-dinners with friends, a day trip to the mountains, plays at our community theater, walks in the neighborhood. Accepting reality, developing a new normal, feeling grateful for my life even with all its challenges, and, above all, being able to laugh at this life's absurdities gave me strength to keep on keeping on.

When I felt centered, I found caregiving to be a spiritual practice. One of my Buddhist teachers described a person's being mindful of whatever she or he was doing and feeling gratitude for the opportunity it presented-even in so mundane a task as washing dishes-as a spiritual practice. He called it Kitchen Yoga. When I could care for Deloris with this consciousness and a feeling of gratitude, I felt engaged in the practice of Kitchen Yoga, although, given Deloris's bladder condition, I renamed it Bathroom Yoga. With this mindset, I was nourished by the depth developing in my own compassion and spirituality. I realized how incredibly blessed our lives were and was grateful for it.

In a workshop entitled "Intentional Spirituality," Rabbi Ted Falcon, our spiritual and religious teacher, said the only way to remove obstacles in one's personal and spiritual evolution is to acknowledge, accept, and feel gratitude for them. Slowly, I was finding the inherent truth in this statement.

I have to admit, however, that as much I valued such moments of mindfulness, they were most often recognized after-the-fact, when I was journaling. In the moment, I was too exhausted by the seemingly endless chores-the necessities that kept the house running-to engage in any metaphysical musings on my life.

One morning, Deloris asked me, "What would make you happy?"

Something in her tone of voice and the way she looked at me when she asked the question brought me up short. When I was engaged in household work, she would often ask if she could help. This was the first time I could remember her posing her inquiry in this more general form. I knew it was a serious question, one grounded in her love. I wanted to respond at the same level of seriousness, but I was caught off guard. I said, "I don't know. Let me think about it. I want to give you the answer the question deserves." She nodded.

The question triggered a cascade of thought. I had no need and no real desire for material objects. New toys were not the answer. The happiness such objects engender is short-lived and superficial. Of course, Deloris's getting back to her former self would bring me a lot of joy, but that would not have been a useful response, as its actualization was out of our control. The question was what would bring me happiness in our life now? Deloris deserved an answer to her question, and I wanted to give one to her.

That I couldn't immediately articulate what made me happy didn't mean I was never happy or was always sad. I wasn't. I usually felt less than whole, but this was more often a passive and reactive experience. Happiness was not a place I had recently dwelt except for very short periods of time-visits, really. Trying to answer Deloris's question triggered an introspection that allowed feelings of loss and the permanent change in my life to surface. Finally, it occurred to me that what mattered most to me were interactions with my wife on a day-by-day basis. The small things.

A few days later, while we were eating breakfast, I said, "Hon, do you remember asking me what would make me happy?"

"Sure," she answered.

"Well, I know the answer. What would make me really happy is for you to cook me a meal, any meal, by yourself. I would be willing to shop for ingredients and help you in the prep, but you would do all the planning and cooking. Seeing you back in the kitchen, and then having the joy of eating what you cooked, would make me happy."

Deloris smiled the crooked, imperfect smile she had since the stroke had altered her ability to control facial muscles. "Me, too."

As she spoke, I glanced out the window and saw the sun breaking through the clouds for the first time in more than a week. That also made me happy.

Once again, I realized how grateful I was for Deloris and for our life together. The key to caring for her brain-injured husband, Alix Kate Shulman writes in her memoir, is amor fati, to love one's fate. My fate with Deloris, our fate together, was pretty damned good. We were blessed in ways we had barely begun to appreciate.

I Was There in the Room

It was a small announcement in the back pages of our Island newspaper: The Vagina Monologues was being produced again locally, and women who wished to try out were encouraged to contact Bev Rose, the producer. Deloris and I had seen Bev's first Whidbey production of the play the year before, and we had both been impressed by the passion and immediacy both Eve Ensler, the playwright, and the local cast members had brought to the words of the monologues. I sent an email to Bev, who by then was a good friend, jokingly protesting the gender specificity in the announcement. Bev responded by saying it was a condition Ensler had set out in licensing the script for local community productions. Even though I couldn't be on stage, if I wanted to be involved, she would find a backstage role I could play.

So began my three-year relationship with The Vagina Monologues, the incredible women involved in the productions, and another creative activity I shared with my wife. I served as stage manager the first two years and co-producer (with Bev) the third. I remember with awe and immense pride the audience's reaction when, the first year we were involved, Deloris, supported by her walker and one of the other performers, slowly crossed to the center of the stage, sat down on a chair in the middle of an empty stage, lit by a spotlight, and said, "I was there in the room . . . ."The audience was silent when she finished her monologue, awed by both the intensity of Ensler's words describing witnessing the birth of her first grandchild and the passion of Deloris's presentation.

My concerns about whether she would be able to deliver her lines-in fact, whether merely walking across the stage was going to be more than she could handle-dissolved into a huge smile of love and pride. I was grateful for the acceptance I felt from the other cast and crew. Even though I was the only man involved in the production, I was happy at the large number of people attending the performances and for the money we raised for the nonprofits supported by ticket sales. Deloris clearly enjoyed being a part of the show, being back working in theater, which had been her college major. I was thrilled she was healthy enough to do so.

Bit by bit, slowly but steadily, my wife was healing, and we were creating a new life together. The two of us were slowly returning to being partners, perhaps not as equal and independent as we had been before Deloris's stroke, but certainly moving in that direction. I was gratified and relieved to be able to relinquish some of my nonstop caregiving and to allow Deloris to make some of her own decisions and, in doing so, expand her capabilities.

Many Expressions of Love

On a number of occasions starting several years after her stroke, Deloris expressed a need for increased intimacy. Our physical relationship had changed dramatically since the stroke. Sex had all but disappeared from our equation. It was more the result of a change in my feelings than any mutual lack of desire. We were no longer equal partners. I found it difficult, if not impossible, to be caregiver, pseudo-parent, and, at the same time, lover. I also had little desire to deal with Deloris's urinary tract infections, a not uncommon result of our prior sexual intimacy. The hassle did not seem worth it, and I did not want to subject Deloris to the discomfort resulting from this condition. This was probably rationalization on my part for some other explanation, but I was disinclined to figure it out. I also rationalized our age, being "senior citizens," had decreased our desires. Yet, I knew there was a difference between a decrease in desire and the absence of sexual feelings.

It was not that I was physically repulsed or averse to contact with Deloris; quite the contrary. I relished our hugs and kisses; I needed them. I just didn't seem to be into sexual contact. In many ways, our connection was more intimate, more soul-full than it had ever been. I felt closer to Deloris than I often had in the past, felt I was relating to her at a much more intimate level. However, that intimacy manifested far differently than it had when Deloris had been well. Though our relationship was now filled with love and tender sharing, it was almost totally devoid of physical passion.

Deloris voiced a need for touch as well. Through discussions with our therapist, we explored whether Deloris's desire for me to help her move about and do things that I knew she was capable of doing herself-things like getting up from a chair or walking from room to room-was really a request for physical touch she did not feel she was getting other ways. Deloris agreed this was probably what she was feeling. I wasn't opposed to touching Deloris, far from it; I was struggling, ineptly at times, to help her be more independent.

I needed to figure out a way to take a breath, think about what was actually happening, and not react to a request for help I found personally inconvenient and thought was unnecessary. I put a note on the wall which read "I would rather give a hug than be a crutch," attempting to remind both of us of the real need being expressed. Deloris responded with "I would rather get a hug than need a crutch." These visual reminders helped us recognize what was happening. When she progressed to the point she could, and did, walk around the house, even up and down the stairs, without much assistance from me, we still both wanted hugs. And we were spontaneous in giving and getting them throughout the day.

Some rituals spontaneously developed. I often awoke earlier than Deloris did in the morning and, after we were able to return to using our second floor bedroom, was downstairs coffee cup in hand when she started down the stairs. I would be standing at the bottom when she reached the last step so we could share a first-in-the-morning-hug and kiss. It was a great way to start our day.

A somewhat similar ritual took place at night. Deloris almost always went to bed earlier than I did. My mother, an insomniac, used to stay up most of the night, a trait my brother inherited. I am not quite that bad, but I seldom get to bed before midnight. Each night after I got into bed, I leaned over and kissed Deloris. If I didn't do so, I felt an emptiness as if some essential part of me was missing.

In the months after her return home from the initial hospital stay, I treasured the time after Deloris went to bed as the only time during the day I considered my own. Parents of young children often share this feeling. Even after Deloris became less dependent on me, I still enjoyed the quiet at night when I was alone after she had gone to bed. At the same time, I looked forward to helping Deloris get into bed: making sure the covers were arranged for her; sharing some quiet, intimate time and a little not-quite-pillow-talk. These were physical expressions of my love for her. I couldn't imagine not being able to "tuck her in" at night. On those periodic nights I was not home when Deloris went to bed, we both felt a little less complete.

So our intimacy was primarily expressed in caresses, hugs, kisses, and my wiping her tush when that was needed, assisting her to take a shower, helping her dress, feeding her, and doing the myriad other things during the course of the day. I didn't question whether it was enough; it was just the way it was. Today I could accept sex was not a major, or even a minor, part of our life. Tomorrow might be different. Maybe even tonight.

Beyond My Wildest Dreams

"Good morning from the cockpit. This is your captain. We are second in line for takeoff. Please make sure your seat belts are fastened. Flight attendants, please prepare the cabin for takeoff."

Jammed into an airplane seat designed for a body other than mine-other than a twenty-first century overfed American male-with Deloris's hand in mine, I half-listened to the captain's announcement. I was elated and feeling a bit overwhelmed. Silently, I mouthed the *sh'ma* prayer I ritually recite when taking off or landing in a plane. In the Jewish tradition, it is the profession of faith you hope to be saying as you die. I was still attempting to take in the full significance of this particular flight: Deloris and I were on our way back to Washington State after being gone for a two-week vacation.

Earlier in the year, Deloris began suggesting we take a trip. I was resistant. Given her physical condition, all I saw were potential difficulties. I had no desire to spend money and energy going somewhere only to be a caregiver in unfamiliar surroundings; it was challenge enough when we were on home turf and sleeping in our own bedroom. The thought of entertaining myself, or being stuck in a hotel room, as Deloris continued her early evening bedtime and late morning risings had little appeal.

I didn't think Deloris had any real concept what the experience would be. Rather, her fantasies were grounded in memories of the enjoyable travels we had taken together before her stroke. I didn't share any of this with my wife, but she definitely noticed my lack of enthusiasm. She tried another tactic. She told me she wanted to go to New York and support Fredericka, who was opening an art exhibit at her New York gallery in October. If I didn't want to go, Deloris said, she would get on a nonstop flight; Fredericka could meet her at the other end. It was a winning ploy. I surprised myself, and Deloris, and agreed to go with her.

Once I'd gone through the mental anguish of deciding to go, I found I was looking forward to the journey. Deloris's strength and mobility had continually improved since her stroke four years before, and especially since she'd started taking Ritalin the year before. If I could manage the logistics, Deloris seemed strong and healthy enough for the journey. We both missed traveling-or at least our memories of traveling-as it had been a major part of our life together before Deloris's stroke.

As such things often do, the trip expanded. Celeste had cancelled her plan to visit us the preceding summer when her husband, Nick, suffered a heart attack. Since we were going to be on the East Coast, Deloris wanted to go a few days early to Rhode Island and visit her daughter.

Our friends Roger and Gayle invited us to join them on a cruise to the Bahamas they had planned to take from the East Coast. Deloris had always liked cruises, and I considered an ocean voyage a particularly easy way to travel with my wife-unpack once, all meals taken care of, and safety not an issue as crews were trained to deal with all sorts of passengers' physical issues. So a cruise to the Bahamas became the third leg of our trip.

Finally, since we were going to be in Miami at the end of the cruise, we would have a chance to see my cousin Phyllis who lived there and was becoming less mobile as she aged. The perfect finale would be to spend a few days with her before flying home.

That's how a long weekend in New York morphed into a two-week journey up and down the East Coast and to the Bahamas. For us this was not unusual travel planning. Before my fiftieth birthday, Deloris asked me where I wanted to go for dinner. I said, "The Oriental Hotel, in Bangkok."

The words surprised me as they came out of my mouth. Deloris's quick "Yeah, we can do that," response surprised me even more. Then, rather than the week in Thailand we had originally envisioned, we spent six weeks in Asia, starting in Nepal and ending in Bali, with stops in Sri Lanka and Thailand along the way. And yes, we did stay at the Oriental for my birthday, although we did not have my celebratory dinner there. We should have, but that's another story. Our present journey developed in similar fashion.

Sitting in the airplane preparing for our flight home, I reflected that this trip had been much easier than I'd expected. I had arranged for wheelchairs and attendants at each airport stop along the way and at Penn Station when we disembarked the train in New York City. Since we had to change planes on every leg of the journey, and sometimes had relatively tight connections, this arrangement made the transfers easier on both of us.

As our plane taxied down the runway, I thought back on all that had happened the preceding two weeks. The trip was, in my mind, an unqualified success. One of my favorite moments occurred in New York. We were with Ben and Fredericka on our way uptown for the evening. We had walked a block from their apartment to Houston Street, a major arterial thoroughfare, where Ben flagged down a cab to take us to the theater. While heading in the right direction, the taxi was, unfortunately, on the other side of the street, and we had to cross six lanes of traffic to reach it. I had some apprehension about Deloris's ability to manage this, but she wasn't worried. She grasped both handles of her walker and, flanked by Fredericka and me, waited for a slight break in the cars. Using her ambulatory device to propel her, Deloris hustled across the street, bumping and pushing that walker in front of her like it was some kind of weaponry. Woe be to the driver who failed to give her room. When the three of us reached the cab Fredericka and I were cheering.

While she may have thought all she had done was cross a street, it was a clear sign to me that Deloris had reached a new level in her recovery. I treasure the mental picture of my wife, woman warrior, risking life and limb to reach a goal, even one as commonplace as crossing a street to catch a cab. In that moment, there seemed to be no limits now to how much more improved Deloris might become.

And in many ways, the question of how much better she might get didn't matter. We were adjusting to our new life together, and I felt buoyed by the currents on which we were, and are now, floating.

November 23, 2009

I think the person who designed the middle seats in airplanes also designed cruise ship cabins. To call our relatively high-priced balcony-cabin on our cruise to the Bahamas "compact" would be generous. My first year in law school, I lived in a graduate dorm building with a roommate. Our room contained two desks and, two single beds, two dressers, arranged with an aisle down the middle just big enough for a person to walk down. There was also one closet. And this dorm room was larger than our cabin. Luckily, in addition to all the necessaries-a queen- sized bed, a closet, some drawers, a desk, couch, TV, and bath-our cabin on the ship included a balcony we could sit out on.

Getting on board was somewhat easy after the nurse cleared us for boarding. I made the mistake of being honest on the medical questionnaire, admitting that we had been coughing and I had a touch of nausea. The cruise line was petrified of H1N1 or other highly communicable diseases. After being assured of the cause of our problems (unusual food, long-standing cough) and learning we had no flu symptoms, the staff gave us a health lecture and allowed us on the ship. Deloris was brought aboard in a wheelchair; I schlepped our carry-ons and her walker. After we'd located the buffet and got a feel for the placement of the bars, we were called for the lifeboat drill. Deloris's condition gave us a reprieve from standing through most of the drill; we were dismissed after we verified our ability to put on lifejackets. There are, it seems, some advantages to traveling with the disabled.

As the cruise got underway, we unpacked and had dinner with our friends Roger and Gayle. Deloris decided to forego evening entertainment in favor of sleep. After making sure she was comfortable, Roger, Gayle and I went to the theater for a surprisingly good show. The cruise director was talented, funny, and had more energy than a hyperactive two-year-old. The guest talent was a magician I had never heard of. I don't remember his actually doing any tricks, but he was extremely funny. Two-for-one martinis and some time in the casino (me as a spectator-one of my favorite things to do in casinos) brought our first evening on board to a close.

The first full day at sea was spent in Freeport, Bahamas. Neither Deloris nor I were feeling up to doing much exploring. Our time in both Newport and

New York had been exciting, but the travel was exhausting. So, we had a delightful day on board: eating, drinking a bit, reading, sleeping, and generally unwinding.

The next day we were in Nassau, and the four of us hired a guide to tour the island. It was fun, and we saw some of the historical sites, but nothing really remarkable. Well, there was the Atlantis Resort, which was remarkable by any definition. Huge, sprawling, the walls of the lower lobby one of many aquariums. After lunch on board, I returned ashore to wander the shopping district-no bargains, except maybe in diamonds and emeralds. Roger bought some Cuban cigars, and I got a straw hat (not a Panama). Deloris opted to have room service for dinner and go to bed early. Roger, Gayle, and I had a wonderful dinner in the ship's small specialty French restaurant. It was nice to be away from the high energy and ambient noise permeating the rest of the ship.

We were supposed to spend the next day enjoying the beach and snorkeling on a small private island the cruise line owned. Unfortunately, the weather had other ideas. We were in the tail end of Hurricane Ida, making the seas too rough for the tenders to get passengers safely to the island. The captain determined we were not to land. And so, we spent a low key, very pleasant day on board. It was a bit windy and cloudy but the seas were not overly rough or nausea inducing. A final dinner with our friends, some evening entertainment, and it was time to pack and get ready for an early morning disembarkation back in Miami.

The passengers were diverse, representing some fifty-plus countries. A large contingent of Latinos, someone said, was predominantly from Argentina. A hundred children were involved in the kids' programs. Deloris saw a crew person wearing a jacket the back of which read "Vice Leader Children's Programs." She wondered what sorts of vices he was leading the kids in but decided not to ask.

All the food was good, and some even slightly better. Although there were no dessert buffets or elaborate ice carvings, there were few hours in which food was not available. In the years since I had been on a cruise, the companies had taken a tip from the airlines and added a bunch of fees-twelve dollars a day per person for tips, fifteen percent service charge on everything, charges for soft drinks. It was not unreasonable, just a bit annoying. There was little to see on shore, but that really didn't matter, as we were there to hang with friends, have some early winter warmth, and relax. In many ways, it was a perfect three-day cruise.

The flights back were long, but blessedly uneventful. Wheelchair pushing assistants again made clearing security, traversing the airport and boarding relatively easy. Again, the plane seats seemed to be made for much smaller people than us, but we survived. Although there was no movie, there was free TV, so we were able to entertain ourselves. A wait of little over an hour for the shuttle and then a two-hour shuttle ride back to the island and we were home. Cold, gray, wet, lovely Whidbey Island.

When I think about what we did the first two weeks in November, I am still amazed. Less than a year ago, I was convinced we would never travel together again. The idea of being responsible not only for myself but also for Deloris; being her caregiver in less than familiar surroundings; dealing with the logistics, hassles, and unexpected problems of traveling were more than I could imagine wanting to assume. Even a couple of days before we left, I remained a bit apprehensive. I knew Deloris's condition had improved far beyond anything I hoped for or imagined possible. She was becoming more independent and mobile; her cognitive abilities had improved, as had her executive functioning. She was still not back to her pre-stroke condition. So, the idea of a vacation, especially one covering as many days and as much territory as we did, was daunting. Luckily, we were with family and close friends at each juncture. This made it easier for me and Deloris, and much more enjoyable as well.

Overall, the trip far exceeded my expectations in every way. Who knows, if we have any money left after paying all the bills for this one, maybe we'll take another journey in the near future.

Allan

EPILOGUE
FLOATING

Building a New Boat

IN THEIR BOOK *The Dude and the Zen Master,* authors Jeff Bridges (the Dude, the character he played in the film *The Big Lebowski*) and Bernie Glassman (a Zen master) discuss how each of us travels through our lives as if on a boat. Surviving certain life situations may require a new kind of boat or a different propulsion system than the one we've been using. As Glassman puts it, "To get to a new, other shore, we have to choose a different path from the first, like getting a different vessel: rowboat, sailboat, dirigible . . . .We choose our vessels and our methods to propel them, which are our practices, to get to where we want to go." When I read this, I thought it described floating with a purpose-not just to stay on top of things but also to propel oneself to a destination.

When I left the shore of my pre-stroke life, however involuntarily, I quickly saw I needed new skills and practices for this challenge, a different vessel if you will, to navigate the rapids and the other unknowns that lay between me and wherever, whatever, that "new, other shore" might be. At the time, I had certain skills and traits. In late 2005, I was a loving partner and spouse, a rational and analytical professional, and a socially active extrovert. This was good, but it wasn't going to be enough. So I learned to construct new vessels, learn new skills, to navigate these new circumstances. In doing so, I learned that while the nature of the vessels one needs may differ, the process by which these needs are identified and the rapids navigated remains the same. This process is what I call floating.

I always become uncomfortable when people tell me how impressed they are that I have taken care of Deloris. I appreciate the comments-I think usually these people are sincere-yet I don't feel I am doing anything so special. I took care of Deloris because, after she had her stroke, it never occurred to me to do anything else. She is my wife. I love her, and in that moment-for those many moments that have followed-she needed me. It is that simple. In considering this question now, I can see I was extremely lucky in my upbringing and in the tradition that forged me. These were the forces that predisposed me to act as I did, and am doing.

My mother was a social worker; my father was a health care professional, more concerned with being of service to his patients than maximizing the earning potential of his profession. My mother worked with survivors of Nazi concentration camps who had relocated to Louisville, our hometown; my father's patients came from the less-affluent groups of society. Though I grew up in the segregated South, I never heard my parents speak derogatorily of Blacks or any other ethnic or political group. Aside from a commitment never to drive a German-made automobile, a common pledge by Jews in the post-war period, I do not remember my parents indicating prejudice of any kind, ever. Through their words and actions, my parents instilled in me a commitment to helping others.

Judaism teaches dedication to *tikkun ha-olam*, the healing of the world. One of the means by which we are to achieve this is by helping those less fortunate, both through contributions to social service organizations and by direct service to or on behalf of individuals and groups of individuals who are in need. By their example, my parents reinforced the lesson of tikkun ha-olam imparted by my religious teachers. It is probably a major reason I spent most of my legal career in the public sector, often representing disadvantaged and oppressed clients. Throughout my adult life, I have devoted my time, energy, and money to a variety of nonprofit, community service organizations.

A combination of these habits, traditions, and teachings, along with the in sickness and in health part of our marriage vows, led me to assume primary care responsibilities for my wife when she became ill. As I've said, it never occurred to me to do otherwise. Had someone asked me before Deloris's stroke how I would respond if and when such a thing occurred, I don't know how I would have answered. I had never even thought about it before. Now, I know what I would do, but only because I've been in the situation. I think it's only in the face of such a situation that anyone ever knows what they will do, what their own mode of response will be.

I don't mean to imply I always faced what was happening with equanimity and acceptance. Far from it. Countless times I cried, screamed in frustration, and cursed in anger at what I perceived as the unfairness of what was happening. There were times, as I've mentioned, when the prospect of an indeterminate future of caregiving seemed more than I could bear to contemplate. These emotions were as real, and often more present, than the compassion, love, and gratitude I also felt. It's all part of what we are, of what makes each of us human. Dealing with our humanity, I feel, is the essence of learning to float.

GUIDELINES FOR FLOATING

AS I WRITE THIS, it has been nine years since Deloris suffered her stroke. I am thankful for the degree to which she has recovered and grateful for our life together, as well as the lessons I have learned from the experience. From needing help with the most basic skills, my wife now accomplishes many things on her own. She moves around the house easily without her cane or walker, although they are both called into use when she tires and whenever she leaves the house. She dresses herself, takes care of her daily toiletry and cleansing routine, is back at her computer writing a new novel. Kitchen activities remain limited, more by a lack of energy than by her previous inability to focus on the cooking process. Deloris's progress in her recovery has made it possible for us to develop a comfortable and enjoyable lifestyle. We travel a bit, go to movies, socialize with friends, and attend lectures, plays, and classes with some regularity. While not exactly as it was before, our present life is far from the nightmare that kept me awake during the early months and years of this journey.

I am aware of how fortunate we have been. Deloris's condition, while debilitating, could have been substantially worse. My family background could have been different, making my transition from rational professional to compassionate caregiver personally more difficult, if not impossible. I am grateful we had financial capacity, supportive friends and family, as well as other resources available. And, whether your situation is similar or totally different, I believe what matters most is intention-to have the mindset and willingness to do what is necessary to navigate the rapids and obstacles on your journey. In short, to have an intention to learn to float.

Over the years, I have identified a dozen precepts I found helpful in this process. I offer them here, in no particular order, in the hope you might find them useful.

- Take care of yourself, first and foremost. Exercise. Eat well. Take naps. Follow a spiritual practice, whatever it might be.

- Look for the positive energy embedded in every event.

- Ask for help. A specific request is a gift to others.

- Laugh. Find the humor in whatever is happening.

- Also cry, shout, and scream. Express your feelings honestly with yourself and others, while always remembering the person you are caring for should not be the object of your anger and abuse.

- Read. Research. Ask questions. Learn all you can about what's happening.

- Share your experiences and lessons with others. Be an inspiration and guide to them as you seek the same from them.

- Be a strong and persistent advocate for your loved one.

- Find intellectual and creative stimulation and social outlets.

- Accept what is happening as the only thing that can be happening. Another way of saying this: Use the current; don't fight it.

- Be thankful for what you have, rather than mourning what you do not have.

- Feel gratitude for the big things of course, but also-especially-for the small.

Writing this book and the emails that preceded it, was one way I gave myself creative and intellectual stimulation. Sharing what I wrote with others helped me maintain social connections and outlets. It has also provided me with a vehicle by which I can share my story and the lessons I learned. I hope others can learn from my journey and that the guidelines I found for floating will serve them-even as they, by necessity, develop their own.

We each face unique circumstances in our lives and often, it follows, distinctive outcomes. Floating is a universal skill. Your attempts to develop that skill may or may not benefit the person you are offering care to, but it will always benefit you, the one who is learning.

Thank you. I feel blessed to have you with me on this journey.

Not Quite the End

Allan Ament
September, 2014

January 17, 2010

A major step forward today, at least it seemed that way to me.

An old friend whom she hadn't seen in decades invited Deloris to lunch in Mukilteo. So, the question was how to get to Ivar's across the street from the Mukilteo ferry terminal. She said she could walk on the boat and then to Ivar's. I was a bit less sanguine about her ability to do it, unaided. I decided to go across with her, get her situated in the restaurant and figure her friend would get her back on the boat.

Things went well with the exception of the ferry's elevator being closed for repair. That meant that Deloris had to walk up two flights of stairs, with about sixteen risers each. At home, our second floor only has fourteen stairs to it and there is a landing after four. This was the most she had climbed in a long time. And with cold metal hand rails as well.

Piece of cake! She did great, although said her legs hurt when we reached the passenger deck. Twenty minutes later, we did it all over again in reverse, and she walked off the ferry, slowly and steadily, her head held high. I decided not to lend support unless it was necessary, as I wanted to see how she did on her own. I was not going to be there on the return trip.

My feelings ran the gamut, from fear something would happen to Deloris, which I could prevent, to joy she felt capable of doing this trip by herself. I didn't rest at either extreme very long, preferring to fluctuate between the two, or merely assume all would work itself out.

I was late picking her up as she took an earlier boat than originally planned and I didn't get the call in time. When I arrived at the terminal, Deloris was sitting on a bench, reading. She said the return voyage was relatively uneventful. One of the ferry workers had helped her onto the boat, (the same broken-elevator vessel we took over), found her a protected and semi-comfortable place to sit on the car deck, and made sure she got off the boat safely. While a bit tired from the journey, Deloris enjoyed the visit and the sense of independence she experienced in making the trip.

I am not sure what any of this means for the future, if it means anything at all. I am extremely glad it all worked out, happy for Deloris to have some personal time and space with friends, and slightly amazed at how far she has progressed. I am learning-we are both learning-to work with her increasing mobility and desire for independence. While I haven't yet gotten back all of her, I see increasingly more and more of the old Deloris returning. I am extremely grateful.

And so, we move into the future with optimism and hope.

Allan

ACKNOWLEDGEMENTS

THIS JOURNEY has provided many lessons, not the least of which is been my learning (yet again) what it meant to feel gratitude from deep within my heart. I know a major danger of thanking specific people is that someone, or more likely more than one, will inevitably be left out. Please understand such omission was definitely not intentional. Rather my memory has decided it likes acting a sieve. So, whether you are named or not, know I am deeply appreciative for the support you provided Deloris and me, in whatever form it appeared.

The idea for *Learning to Float* originated in a series of emails that were sent to friends and family; to those of you who received these emails and encouraged me to turn them into a book, many thanks. I probably would never have done so had it not been for your urging.

Both Deloris's and my family provided help despite being spread from one end of the country to the other. Celeste, Ginnie and Hans, David and Ruth, Karen and Larry (of blessed memory), Jeslyn, Mark and Sue, Aaron, Rachel, thank you. Even though the closest any of you live is over 1000 miles away in Salt Lake City and you all had your own lives and hardships with which to contend, y'all were there when we really needed you, and often when we didn't.

To my parents, Milton and Bernice Ament, of blessed memory, I am grateful for all the love and lessons they gave me. I hope I made you proud.

To Roger and Gayle, mahalo, and eight letters.

Ben and Fredericka, you have been with us from the start of our relationship, brought insight and creativity to our housing problem, fed us, gave us shelter in the Big Apple, and loved us throughout. Thank you.

To my Circle of Caring members, Roger, Margaret, Mark, Effie, Kate, Gaea, Johnny, Yvonne, Bernie, Gretchen, Cynthia, and Barbara, I appreciate the love, the support, the laughter, and the potlucks. And special thanks to Barbara for teaching me asking for help is giving a gift.

Leah Green, thank you for being part of our life and journey. You have helped us more than you can imagine. Rebecca Ruby, the same is true for you. I am grateful for both of you.

This book would never have been written without the encouragement and instruction from my writing teachers, Sheila Bender and Molly Cook, (not to mention Mrs. Scott, my eleventh grade English teacher), the suggestions of the Wednesday afternoon TLC writers group, the members of Laptop Writers, and Andrea Hurst. Jane Adams' feedback was valuable, while her friendship, love, and support over the years are even more so. Thank you. I am incredibly grateful to Margaret Bendet for her expertise in providing editorial guidance in the shaping of this book. Your professionalism, Margaret, is matched only by your compassion. I am grateful to Lori A. May for your confidence in this project and your assistance in getting it out to the public.

Jesse James Freeman, the BookTrope staff and my BT team, Patricia Eddy, Julie Simrock, Cecile Jagodzinski, and Melody Barber. Y'all are the greatest. Terry Persun, thanks.

Hestia, the staff and volunteers at the Island County Senior Center and Time Together, Marti Murphy, Sari Spieler, Natalie Pace, Deloris's physical, speech and occupational therapists, Tom Harris, Kathleen Kobashi, Eric Gierke, and the other members of Deloris's medical team, I am indebted to your efforts and perseverance in helping Deloris improve.

My colleagues in the School of Advanced Studies, University of Phoenix, provided friendship, intellectual conversation, laughter, and help. Thanks. I needed it.

Deloris and I are indeed blessed to live on South Whidbey Island, in the midst of compassionate community. I am grateful every day when I awake on this beautiful island. Yes, it does take a village.

To Ram Dass, Ken Wilber, Alix Kate Shulman, Abigail Thomas, and the other authors whose books gave me inspiration, motivation, and information, thank you. Similarly, to Groucho, Harpo, and Chico for getting me through some dark nights.

To everyone at the Northwest Institute of Literary Arts, just because . . .

Carlyle, Lydia, Kona, and Chiza, you have been important in our lives and this journey.

I am so grateful to my loving and lovely wife, Deloris, for everything. Without your presence in it, this life would be far less enjoyable. For all your love, for all the lessons you have taught me intentionally and otherwise, for your intelligence, your heart, your commitment to get better, and for putting up with me when I act in ways I have no business acting, I am incredibly grateful. I love you more than I can express.

SELECTED RESOURCES

Below is a list of resources-memoirs, books on care-giving, websites, and other material I found useful along my journey. This is far from a complete list of what is available and I encourage you to do your own research. It is meant only as a starting point that includes some items I found useful.

Memoir

Alford, Henry. *How to Live: A Search for Wisdom from Old People (While They are Still on this Earth).* New York: Twelve Books, 2009.
Memoir and interviews with the elderly about the wisdom gained from them.

Bayley, John. *Elegy for Iris.* New York: St. Martin's Press, 1999.
Memoir of author's marriage to and life together with Iris Murdoch.

Beaver, Jim. *Life's That Way: A Memoir. New York:* Amy Einhorn Books, 2009.
Memoir, based on emails to friends, written by Hollywood author about the death of his wife from cancer and his subsequent life with a young autistic daughter.

Bruschi, Tedy and Michael Holley. *Never Give Up: My Stroke, My Recovery, and My Return to the NFL*. Hoboken, NJ: John Wiley, 2007.
  Inspiring personal story by professional football player.

Casey, Neil, ed. *An Uncertain Inheritance: Writers on Caring for Family*. New York: William Morrow, 2007.
  Anthology of personal stories of caregiving by well-known authors.

Cooney, Eleanor. *Death in Slow Motion: My Mother's Descent into Alzheimer's*. New York: Harper Collins, 2003.
  Stories of caregiving for mother for the two years before her death from Alzheimer's, with some emphasis on personal impact on both caregiver and her partner.

Cousins, Norman. *Anatomy of an Illness Perceived by the Patient*. New York: Norton, 1979.
  Editor of Saturday Review discusses importance of laughter as healing power.

Desserich, Brooke and Keith Desserich. *Notes Left Behind*. New York: William Morrow, 2009.
  Parents' memoir of child's struggle with and ultimate death from pediatric brain cancer, based on daily journal entries.

Didion, Joan. *The Year of Magical Living*. New York: Vintage Books, 2006.
  Author's memoir of year after hospitalization of daughter and death of husband.

Douglas, Kirk. My Stroke of Luck. New York: William Morrow, 2002.
  Actor's story of recovery from stroke.

Ram Dass. *Still Here: Embracing Aging, Changing, and Dying*. New York: Riverhead Books, 2000.
  Advice about aging and post-stroke memoir from spiritual teacher.

Rieff, David. *Swimming in a Sea of Death: A Son's Memoir*. New York: Simon & Schuster, 2008.
Susan Sontag's son writes of his mother's death.

Romm, Robin. *The Mercy Papers: A Memoir of Three Weeks*. New York: Scribner, 2009.
Author was part of care-giving team for mother's last days. Book focuses on emotional and personal impact experienced by author.

Shulman, Alix Kates. *To Love What Is: A Marriage Transformed*. New York: Farrar, Strauss, & Giroux, 2008.
Beautifully written memoir of caring for previously active husband for first two years after he suffered traumatic brain injury from a fall.

Taylor, Jill Bolte. *My Stroke of Insight*. New York: Viking, 2008.
A Harvard neuro-anatomist writes of lessons learned from suffering massive stroke.

Thomas, Abigail. *A Three Dog Life*. New York: Harcourt, 2006.
Importance of her dogs in helping maintain emotional stability for years after husband suffered traumatic brain injury.

Wilber, Ken. *Grace and Grit: Spirituality and Healing in the Life and Death of Treya Killam Wilber*. Boston: Shambala, 1991.
Weeks after she and Ken were married, Treya Wilber was diagnosed with terminal cancer. The book is part he said/she said journal from Wilber and his wife and part philosophical musings on life and love as the couple embark on a multi-year journey ending in Treya's death.

Books on Caregiving

Clarke, Jean Illsey and Connie Dawson. *Growing Up Again: Parenting Ourselves, Parenting our Children*. Center City, MN: Hazelden, 1998.
    Therapists discuss how the elderly and brain-damaged revert back to childhood stages of development.

Hay, Jennifer. *Stroke: Questions You Have . . . Answers You Need*. Allentown, PA: People's Medical Society, 1995.
    Good information on strokes presented in easy to read question-and-answer form.

Stein, Joel, Silver, Julie, and Elizabeth Pegg Frates. *Life After Stroke: The Guide to Recovering Your Health & Preventing Another Stroke*. Baltimore: Johns Hopkins University Press, 2006.
    Good basic information on strokes.

Inspirational Books

Baldwin, Christina. Storycatcher: Making Sense of Our Lives Through the Power and Practice of Story. Novato, CA: New World Library, 2005.
    Importance of personal stories as part of the human fabric.

Bridges, Jeff and Bernie Glassman. *The Dude and the Zen Master*. New York: Blue Rider Press, 2012.
    Dialogue between actor and spiritual leader on the importance of doing good in a difficult world.

Matousek, Mark. *When You're Falling, Dive*. New York: Bloomsbury USA, 2008.
    Series of interviews with people, famous and not, who have endured and learned from life-changing experiences.

Ram Dass. *Still Here: Embracing Aging, Changing, Dying.* New York: Riverhead Books, 2000.
Advice on aging and the meaning of life from an American teacher of Eastern spiritual tradition who suffered a massive stroke during the writing.

Websites

Using key words such as stroke or caregiving in any search engine will result in links to numerous websites, many containing useful information and resources. Those listed below are just a few of the ones I found, and used, in my research. I have not included any of the medically oriented sites, such as mayoclinic.com/health/stroke or stroke.ahaournals.org

AARP.org - website has good information and resources for caregiving, accessible for non-members as well as association members.

www.americanheart.org - has statistics on stroke occurrences and information of value to caregiver, even though stroke is not a heart-related medical issue

Caregiving.com - website of the National Alliance for Caregiving-good resources although focused primarily on Alzheimer's and MS

Caringbridge.org - "an online space where you can connect, share news, and receive support." Includes personalized sites for connecting with friends and family during health event as well as support planner/calendar for organizing help

Care-givers.com - website includes chat rooms, resources, lists of experts, suggested readings and other information to help empower caregivers

Caregiver.com - website of the Caregiver Media Group, which publishes Today's Caregiver, a newsletter, and other resources "developed for caregivers, about caregivers, and by caregivers." Site contains a state-by-state map of resources and valuable information on a variety of subjects

Lotsahelpinghands.com - websites similar to CaringBridge sponsored by Empowering Caregivers organization

Strengthforcaring.com - Sponsored by Johnson & Johnson, website contains good information on variety of subjects of interest to caregivers and links to resources

Stroke.org - site of the National Stroke Association, a non-profit dedicated to increasing public awareness of stroke, its prevention, treatment, and support for those impacted by stroke

Strokeassociation.org - companion site of the American Heart Association with information and resources on stroke-little focus on caregiving

Strokenetwork.net -- contains resources specific to concerns of stroke survivors and caregivers of adults experiencing stroke

ABOUT THE AUTHOR

After successful careers as a criminal defense attorney, higher education administrator and instructor, and day spa owner, Allan Ament now enjoys retirement in Freeland with his wife Deloris, an award-winning author and journalist, and their cat. They live on an island in the Salish Sea, north of Seattle, Washington. In addition to writing and being his wife's caregiver, Ament is active in local non-profit organizations. His writing has previously appeared in academic, professional, and literary journals, and is included in the anthology, *Being: What Makes a Man*. *Learning to Float* is his first book-length work.

OTHER BOOKS FROM
ABIDING NOWHERE PRESS

Bite Into the Day: One Day at a Time, a book of poetry by Miriam Sonn Raabe

Enso House: Caring for Each Other at the End of Life, by David Daiku Trowbridge

In Awe of Being Human: A Doctor's Stories from the Edge of Life and Death, by Betsy McGregor, M.D.

Speak Up for a Child: Reflections of a Lifelong Teacher, by Jeanne R. Strong

Take Care of Dying Get On with Living: End-of-Life Planning that Works, by Theo Wells

Abiding Nowhere Press
www.abidingnowhere.com

60362419R00118

Made in the USA
Lexington, KY
04 February 2017